Preaching for Growth

by Ronald J. Allen

CBP Press
St. Louis, Missouri

© 1988 CBP Press

CBP Press, Box 179, St. Louis, MO 63166.

Library of Congress Cataloging-in-Publication Data

Allen, Ronald J.
      Preaching for growth / by Ronald J. Allen.
           p. cm.
      ISBN 0-8272-2941-0 : $5.95
      1. Preaching.   I. Title.
BV4211.2.A39   1988   87-25664
251—dc19   CIP

Printed in the United States of America

For
GENESIS
First Born Daughter
in Whose Name Is Our Confidence
That God Has Made a New Beginning for Women
in Our Time

Contents

Introduction

Studies of growing congregations consistently point to a strong, positive relationship between church growth and preaching.[1] In growing churches, people find the preaching (and the service of worship) to be interesting, meaningful, alive, and even life-giving. Week after week, the members of the congregation leave the sanctuary feeling that the service of worship has made a positive difference in their lives. Nourished in the gospel, they are strengthened for life and witness.

The purpose of this book is to identify important characteristics of Christian preaching that can make this kind of difference in human lives. By so doing, it will contribute to the growth of the church.

Of course, one can preach in such a way that the church grows but the gospel of God is neither proclaimed nor received. In a world hungry for meaning and hope, people will turn to anything that promises a way forward. And from the pulpits of growing (as well as non-growing) churches all across the land, one can hear everything from pop psychology, to political bigotry, to license for human abuse. But such preaching is not Christian preaching. It is falsehood made doubly heinous because it has been blessed by gown and pulpit.

Thus, we need always to remember that the criterion of Christian preaching is not its contribution to church growth but its faithfulness to God. The preacher's business is to tell the truth. It so happens that Christian truth is of such a character that its telling will ultimately cause the church to grow.

The reader will not find here a formula for a special kind of "evangelistic preaching." Rather, the underlying conviction is that faithful parish preaching will contribute to the growth of the church. The Christian pastor nurtures weekly the congregation in the gracious love of God. Secure in that love, the people respond in joyful faith, in praise and thanksgiving to God, and in lives of love and justice. A congregation built on this foundation can fulfill the purpose of the church: to witness to the presence, purpose, and power of God in the world. Indeed, this church can be a light to the nations.

While twenty characteristics of Christian preaching are proposed in this booklet, no attempt is made to resolve all of the basic issues in sermon preparation. For example, the decisions about whether a sermon should be basically expository or thematic, inductive or deductive, are important decisions and should be carefully made. But a sermon developed on any organizing principle can be an effective witness to the gospel if it is controlled by a lively, responsible theology and if it is prepared and delivered with conviction, good sense, pastoral care, and sensitivity to life. The characteristics of preaching outlined here can be manifest in any form of Christian preaching.

Preachers might want to read this book alongside a representative group of their sermons. Read the book and then go through the sermons, looking for the presence (or absence) of the twenty characteristics. To help with this process, the author has ended each section with a question or exercise that can be put to any sermon. With an accurate picture in mind, the preacher can begin systematically strengthening his or her preaching. The book concludes with a summary list of the questions and with a brief, annotated bibliography of some important books on preaching.

Before turning to the characteristics of Christian preaching, we will be helped by an overview of the relationship of preaching, evangelism, and church growth. We will see that church growth is a sub-category of evangelism and that preaching is evangelistic when it brings the gospel of God to bear on the lives of particular individuals and communities. This perspective asks preachers to see themselves as the bearers of good news. To use the evocative image of Second Isaiah, preachers are heralds whose feet are beautiful upon the mountains because of the news that they carry, "Your God reigns!"(Isaiah 52:7).

The author wishes to thank several persons who directly and indirectly have contributed to this project. Herb Miller, Director of the National Evangelistic Association, suggested that these thoughts be put into print. My brother-in-law, Professor John E. McKiernan of the University of South Dakota, read the whole manuscript with a discerning eye. Others who have read parts of the piece are the Reverend Charles R. Blaisdell and the Reverend Barbara Shires Blaisdell of Monahans, Texas, as well as Professors Keith Watkins, D. Newell Williams, and Clark M. Williamson of Indianapolis, and Professor Linda Schearing of Atlanta. Joy Sherrill typed the manuscript. While the author is grateful for their guidance, the author alone is responsible for the content of the work.

Ronald J. Allen
Christian Theological Seminary
Indianapolis, Indiana, U.S.A.

Preaching As Evangelism: The Big Picture

Preaching is a form of evangelism. In popular use, the word "evangelism" has come to be synonymous with adding members to the church. But a recollection of the origin and use of the larger meaning of evangelism will reveal that evangelism is much more than church growth. Of course, where evangelism is taking place, the church may be expected to grow and its faithful witness to increase. Our English word "evangelism" is derived from the Greek root *euangel*, which appears in the Bible as a verb and as a noun.[2] The word is composed of two parts: (1) The root *angel* refers to a message, a messenger, or the activity of delivering a message; (2) The prefix *eu* denotes the quality of goodness and thus identifies the nature of the message and the messenger. As a noun, the word *euangellion* is a message of good news, and as a verb *euangelizo* refers to the act of bringing good news.

In the English versions of the Bible, the words taken from this root are usually translated into terms like "gospel" (e.g., Matthew 4:23, Romans 1:16), "to preach good news" (e.g., Luke 4:18, Romans 10:15), "to preach" (e.g., Galatians 1:16), "evangelist" (e.g., Ephesians 4:11). As can be seen from its frequent occurrence in the letters of Paul and other early writings, the early church quickly began to use the word "gospel" as a summary of its central message. While the precise meaning and content of these words can only be determined by examining their use by particular authors in specific contexts, they all denote the quality of good news.

In the Hebrew Scriptures we find a rich background.[3] In time of military conflict, the "evangelist" can be a messenger who comes from the front line where the battle has been raging and brings the news of victory to those who cannot see what has taken place.

9

In Psalm 68, a hymn of victory, God is pictured as marching through history. Faithful to the divine character and promises, God delivers the people of Israel from all manner of oppression and want. In vs. 11-12, the Psalmist cries out,

> The Lord gives the command;
>> great is the host who bore the tidings (i.e., good news):[4]
>> "The kings of the armies, they flee, they flee!"

By nothing more than the power of the word of God (!), the enemies of Israel are scattered. The evangelists come running with the news of God's victory.

Isaiah 40-55 was delivered during one of the most painful moments in the history of Israel: the exile in Babylon. Defeated, the leadership of the community was uprooted from Jerusalem and marched across the baking desert to live as refugees in alien Babylon. Economically and politically impotent in Babylon, they were surrounded by a nation that spoke a strange language, ate strange food, and worshiped strange gods. Worse, the community was estranged from the symbols of the steadfastness of God, especially the land and the temple.

For exiles, Isaiah pictures the role and message of the evangelist and the response of the community.

> How beautiful upon the mountains
>> are the feet of him who brings good tidings,
> who publishes peace, who brings good tidings of good,
>> who publishes salvation,
>> who says to Zion, "Your God reigns."
> Hark, your watchmen lift up their voice,
>> together they sing for joy, for eye to eye they see
>> the return of the Lord to Zion.
>>> (Isaiah 52:7-8, cf. 40:9, 41:27)

Evangelism means bringing the news of the deliverance from exile. Homecoming is beginning. To a community in chaos, evangelism is saying to Zion, "Your God reigns." No wonder the lookouts lift up their voices and sing for joy.

The same pattern is found in the canonical writings of the early church. As in the case of the Hebrew scriptures, the specific content of the good news is often stated differently from author to author.[5] God's gracious love is not divided in nature or in intention, of course, but the one love is perceived in different ways according to the circumstances of different communities.

For instance, a major belief of the world in which the Gospel of Mark was written was the division of history into two epochs. One was the existing order, marked by the freewheeling, crippling power of Satan and the demons, which was soon to pass away. The other was the coming sovereign domain (RSV: kingdom) of God. For Mark, the good news (1:14, gospel) is that the "sovereign domain of God is near" (1:15). Evangelism is carrying the news that Jesus, who died on the cross and was raised from the dead, is the stronger one who has already overcome the power of Satan and the demons (e.g., 3:19-26).

For the world of Paul's churches, a major concern was alienation from the power(s) that controlled the universe. Indeed, the hellenistic culture in which Paul preached was beset with deep, enervating anxiety. One reason for this anxiety was a popular belief that life was under the power of blind, unchangeable fate. By nothing more than the caprice of fate, one could receive a meaningless life of unredeemed suffering. In this setting, Paul announces that one can be in right relationship (i.e., justified) with the fundamental power of the universe, God. By the death and resurrection of Jesus, all are justified by grace through faith (e.g., Romans 3:21-26) and, as a result, can live in peace (e.g., Romans 5:1-5). In fact, God is not capricious. God is for us (Romans 8:31). As the letter to the Romans moves toward its peak, Paul speaks eloquently of the importance of preaching by drawing on Isaiah 52:7 in Romans 10:15.

In each of these examples, the specific content of the good news is focused for the particular community to whom it is given.

—For Israel in conflict, the good news is the announcement that God has caused the enemy to flee.

—For Israel in exile, the good news is that God is beginning the homecoming.

—For a world choking in the grip of Satan, the good news is that Jesus is the stronger one.

—For a world alienated from the gods, the good news is that reconciliation with God has been revealed in Jesus Christ.

Despite the differences of emphasis in these manifestations of the good news of God, all are underlaid by a consistent revelation of

God's gracious, faithful, loving character. And in each case, the telling of the news is evangelism.[6]

By lifting up good news as the fundamental character of Christian preaching, have we turned away from the tradition of prophetic critique and challenge? Many of the classical prophets spoke sharply and powerfully against sin and injustice in ways that hardly sound like "good news." In the Gospel of Matthew, for instance, Jesus himself is depicted as belonging to this tradition when he refers to the prevalent religious community as "blind guides" and "whitewashed tombs" (Matthew 23:24, 27).

We need always to remember that the prophetic preaching of judgment takes place within the framework of the covenant.[7] The covenant is founded upon the promise of God's gracious love and sets forth appropriate responses to that love in the form of covenantal stipulations. To use the language of Deuteronomy, when the community responds to the love of God by living according to the stipulations of the covenant, it is blessed. When it violates its relationship with God as expressed in the covenant, it falls under the curse (e.g., Deuteronomy 28).

A major role of the prophet is to read the signs of the times in the light of the covenant and to discern the word that the community needs to hear.[8] According to James A. Sanders, the prophet operates along an axis that has two poles: constitution and challenge. At a given moment, the prophet decides whether the community needs the constitutive (encouraging) word or the challenging word. If the community doubts the love, promises, faithfulness, and power of God, then the prophet speaks to reassure the community. Second Isaiah, for instance, begins with the words, "Comfort, comfort my people . . . ." If the community is confident of the love, promises, faithfulness, and power of God, but is responding inappropriately to these things, then the prophet challenges the community to conform its life to the character of the covenant. The prophet reminds the community that they are graciously loved by God and need now to live in ways consistent with that love.[9] Two recurring problems in the life of Israel (and one might suggest that they are recurring in the life of the church today) were the turning to false gods and the neglect (and even active maltreatment) of the poor. The prophet always speaks as a member of the community and not as an "outsider." Prophetic self-criticism became a living part of the Jewish community.

Whether speaking in the mode of constitution or in the mode of challenge, the purpose of the prophet is to build up the life of the community. In this sense, even prophetic critique has good news as its ultimate goal.[10]

Thus, to claim that Christian preaching has the basic character of evangelism is not to say that the preacher winks at sin and injustice. Still less does the preacher "tell the people what they want to hear" or reduce the gospel to an uncritical massage of the middle-class ego. It is instead to say that the preacher's starting point is the good news of God's gracious, faithful love for all, a love that is expressed afresh not only in every generation and circumstance but in every moment of every day. The preacher's calling is to announce the unconditional claim of that love on the world and to show how it can transform every person and situation.

While space will not permit an extensive survey, a look at representative figures in the history of the church and in the modern era will show that preaching has consistently been understood as bearing witness to the good news of God. Augustine, for instance, saw the goal of the sermon as to awaken the hearers to the love of God for them. In response, the hearers will love God and neighbor.[11]

According to Luther, nothing except Christ is to be preached from the Christian pulpit. By this, Luther means that the sermon is to assure the listeners that they have been saved (accepted by God) by grace. Only by trusting in the grace of God can the soul come to rest. "Whoever, therefore, does not know or preach the gospel is not only no priest or bishop, but he is a kind of pest to the church. . . ."[12] In similar fashion, Calvin saw the purpose of preaching as to cause the gospel to flourish.[13]

Alexander Campbell, a progenitor of the Christian Church (Disciples of Christ), distinguished between two kinds of public discourse. One, called preaching, was intended for the unconverted and designed to set forth the facts and testimony of the gospel in a rational and coherent way so that listeners would choose to believe.[14] The other, called teaching, was essentially the exposition of the Bible for the sake of building up the established congregation in the gospel.[15] The former took place largely outside of the Sunday assembly. The latter was the focus of the main discourse on Sunday morning.[16]

For Barton Stone, another leader in the early 1800s on the

U.S. frontier, preaching exposed the human situation apart from God as hopeless and pointed the sinner to Christ as the source of salvation.[17] In his autobiography Stone described hearing the sermon that ended his struggle and brought him to peace and purpose. The preacher spoke of "the Love of God to sinners, and of what that love had done for sinners." At that, Stone's heart "warmed with love for that lovely character described . . . ."[18]

Summarizing the implications for evangelism in the thought of several major theologians in the middle of the 20th century, Pieter de Jong notes, "Sharing one's faith does not mean adding another organization to people's already overburdened lives, but asking them to open their eyes to God, who is with them even in the places where they would least expect. . . ." Evangelism, and hence preaching, is pointing to "the outgoing love of God which alone can make life full and give it roots in an age of rootlessness. It aims at true community."[19] Those who are filled with the "spirit of gratitude for God's love" will respond with lives of discipleship.

While not writing under the rubric of evangelism, a major Disciples theologian of our time offers an understanding of the gospel and of preaching which follows in the tradition of the church, is consistent with Disciples' beliefs, and is informed by the modern world.[20] Says Clark Williamson, the gospel is the "good news that God graciously and freely offers the divine love to each and all (oneself included) and that this God who loves all creatures therefore commands that justice be done to them." The preacher articulates the promise of the love of God in the light of the specific situation of the hearers and shows how the acceptance of that love both renews the lives of all who accept it and issues in a life of justice for all. Such preaching is a form of evangelism and will likely result in the growth of the church and, hence, its witness.

The first responsibility of Christian preachers is to come to a clear and concise understanding of the content of the gospel and of their roles as witnesses.[21] What, then, are the characteristics of Christian preaching that can help the gospel message become truly news and truly good for the modern listener? We propose twenty such distinguishing marks.

14

1. God Is at the Center of the Sermon

The subject of Christian preaching is God and God's relationship with the world. While this may seem self-evident, it is possible today to hear from the pulpit informed, provocative, helpful, even eloquent discussions of important matters without explicit (or even implicit) reference to God. Things like sociology, psychology, economic and political analysis, community affairs, and institutional promotion can become the functional center of the sermon. One occasionally hears a sermon so void of religious sentiment that it could be given comfortably by an atheist.

Two factors coincide to point to the necessity of God being the center of the sermon. One is the nature of the gospel itself: it is good news from God for the sake of the redemption of the world. The other is the reason people come to church: they come to be touched by God.[22]

When people seek legal advice, they go to a lawyer. When they seek medical diagnosis, they go to a physician. When people seek encounter with God, they come to church. The preacher is a theologian, one whose calling is to interpret the significance and nature of God for the life of the world.

In the sermon, then, the preacher talks about life in the light of God and about God in the light of life. Anything from art history to zoology which helps us understand life or God is a proper contributor to the sermon, as long as it is brought into the sermon in the service of the gospel.

Further, the sermon needs to make responsible statements about God and God's relationship to the world. Two criteria for the claims made in the sermon are especially important: appropriateness and intelligibility.[23]

To be *appropriate*, the sermon's statements about God and God's relationship with the world need to be consistent with the nature of God and the content of the gospel. For example, the fundamental conviction of the gospel is that God loves the world.

15

As Clark Williamson delightfully says,

> God does not just love you and me; God loves all the creatures in what is a rather large universe. God loves the flora and the fauna, the sparrows do not die unnoticed, and certainly, therefore, God loves all those strange people—Russians, Falasha (black) Jews of Ethiopia, Iranians, New Yorkers, southern Californians, women, blacks, Asians, native Americans, WASPs, Jews who aren't black, Yuppies—every kind of odd duck in this pluralistic world. God loves the ecosystem, the biosphere, the people, the past with all its treasures, the present with its vivacity, the future with its possibilities.[24]

In preaching, therefore, it is inappropriate to say that anyone or anything is outside the embrace of God's love. When the church or those in the world accept the idea that anyone or anything is beyond the love of God, the result can be disaster and death. For example, German Nazis (most of whom were baptized Christians) widely believed that Jews were beyond the love of God. It was only a small step from that belief to the holocaust. So it is important to question the sermon's appropriateness. Is the content of the sermon appropriate to the gospel?

The sermon also needs to be *intelligible*. Does the claim of the sermon make sense in view of the modern understanding of the universe and of God? Can we believe what the sermon says about God and about God's activity in the world without suspending what we otherwise know to be true? Is the sermon's claim about the world, about God, and about God's relationship to the world consistent with the claims made about these matters in other sermons and in other arenas of the life of the church?

Take the case of prayer. Suppose the preacher makes the bald claim that everything asked in prayer in the name of Jesus will be done on earth. So, the child goes home and prays (in the name of Jesus) for a bicycle. In the dark night, a tornado tears at a house and from the basement a terrified woman pleads, "Stop it, God! Stop it!" A husband prays for God to cause his wife, who is dying of cancer, to recover.

The preacher has offered the congregation an understanding of God. The congregation has accepted that understanding and acted upon it. Yet, there is no bicycle on the porch. The tornado turns the house into matchsticks. A doctor says, "I'm sorry. We did everything we could." The preacher created conditions for the erosion of trust between the congregation and God, as well as between the congregation and him or herself.[25] The good news has curdled into bad news.

Clearly, then, the fundamental preparation for evangelistic preaching is to come to clarity and conviction about God and God's relationship to the world. Then, the preacher will have a theological yardstick with which to measure every sermon.

In our time, it is important that the sermon bring a word not only *from* God but also *about* God. In the world in which we live, it is not obvious that God exists. And if we can believe that God does exist, what is the character of this God? Contradictions between the suffering of the world and traditional Christian affirmations about the love, power, and justice of God are often so great as to cast in doubt both the nature and the existence of God. The contradictions of experience combine with our increasingly sophisticated knowledge of the universe to make belief difficult. For many, as Gordon Kaufman says, God is the problem.[26] Edmund A. Steimle puts the matter graphically. "How can you believe in a good and loving God in a hell of a world like this?"[27] Therefore, a key component of evangelism is helping the congregation understand why it can believe in God, as well as to understand the kind of God in whom it trusts.

Diagnostic Question

1. What does this sermon say about God?
   a. Is it appropriate to the gospel?
   b. Is it intelligible?

2. Christian Preaching Has the Character of Good News

In the study of language, a recurrent emphasis is placed on the importance of image, metaphor, and name. For the images, metaphors, and names we use to describe things, people, and activities shape our perception of those realities and our behavior in the light of them.[28] We tend to become what we imagine (image) ourselves to be.

From this perspective, it is critical for Christian preachers to perceive themselves as bearers of good news and to perceive their sermons as messages of good news. As we think, so we become.

This perception is important for at least three reasons. First, as we have already discovered, the gospel itself is fundamentally good news. In order for the sermon to be appropriate to the content of the gospel, the sermon will manifest the same character.

Second, in the world in which we live, the notion of "preaching" is frequently perceived in a negative way. In a Sunday school class with lay people, I recently posed the question, "When you hear the word 'preach,' what first comes to mind?" Few of the responses were fully positive. Most of the people in this group thought of preaching as dull, irrelevant, being told what to do and think. One person responded, "When I think of preaching, I think of my mother shaking her finger at me and telling me a lot of stuff I don't want to hear." Another replied, "I think of hearing my dad say to my mother, 'Don't you preach to me!'" Even if preachers do not shake their fingers at congregations, they may unconsciously think of preaching as little more than passing out free moral advice or even as an exercise in insignificance. Sermons informed by such images only reinforce the pattern of perception and response exemplified in the Sunday school class. This works not only against the sermon but against the gospel itself.

Third, the tone and content of the sermon affects the congregation's view of and confidence in God. If the sermon is interesting, sensible, passionate, and lifts up a large and loving God who relates graciously not only to "the world" but to the congregation, then the congregation will come to have confidence in that God and will reflect the character of that God in daily living. But if the sermon is dull, unorganized, a chore to listen to, and (worse) focused on a narrow, rigid, bookkeeping God, the congregation will come to believe that God is dull, chaotic, small, and preoccupied with retributive judgment.

The congregation's view of God will ultimately affect its sense of mission in the world and even the quality of its own life. A small-minded God begets small-minded people, for whom a major issue in life may be the color of the restroom under the basement stairs. A large and gracious God yields a people who say, "The world is our parish."

Oddly, preaching good news is hard work. The preacher will nearly always find it easier to talk about the bad news of the world's condition than to point specifically and concretely to the renewing power of God. This is particularly true at the point of illustration. It is usually much easier to illustrate sin, brokenness, or injustice than it is to illustrate the grace, love or providential care of God. It is easier to whine, scold, and nag church members than it is to think carefully and creatively about ways in which the love of God can be offered to them so they will want to respond in ways consistent with that love. Yet the nature of the gospel, as well as the principle that images shape our perception of reality and our behavior, insists that the sermon have the basic character of good news.

Please do not misunderstand. This is not a call to retreat from prophetic critique or to deny the cross. Still less is it giving license to ignore sin, gloss over honest guilt, or give false comfort to the cruel. Preaching that does not have the cross as its heart or that pats cruel people on the back and sends them out the door only to continue their cruelty is not good news. At best it is shallow optimism and at worst complicity with cruelty and a gross misrepresentation of God. But the Christian preacher is not content to dwell neurotically on the cross or to expose cruelty. The preacher's ultimate goal is to show how God's suffering love on the cross is good news, even for the cruel.

The preacher steps into the pulpit on Sunday morning bearing the greatest gift the congregation will ever receive. The purpose of the sermon is to unwrap the gift and to ask, "Now, what are we going to do with it?"[29]

Diagnostic Question

2. In this sermon, what is the good news from God for the congregation?

3. Preaching Relates the Gospel to Real Life

Preaching interprets life from the perspective of the gospel. Indeed, the effectiveness of preaching increases proportionately to the degree that the issues, questions, and situations in the sermon are of genuine concern to the congregation and to the world.

The basic issue in life is meaning. From those who painted on cave walls to those who paint on subway halls, basic questions are asked in every generation. Who are we? Why are we here? On what can we depend in this cosmos? What are we to do? What does it all mean? Preaching becomes a form of evangelism when it helps the congregation make sense of its life in the world.[30]

The fundamental clue to the meaning of life is found in relationship with God. If this relationship is secure, a person or community can make its way among other issues. In grace, God offers unmerited, unending, divine love to the world. When we trust in that love as all-sufficient to establish the value, purpose, and meaning of life, we find the all-sufficient security to look at every issue in life from the perspective of the loving purpose of God and to live no longer for ourselves but for God. When we fail to trust in God, we are left to secure our own existence. Often, through falsehood, manipulation, and oppression, we are willing to ask other people (and the creation itself) to pay a high price for our self-created security. Thus, Christian preaching needs to deal regularly and creatively with this fundamental matter.

Other important concerns, personal and social, are usually symptoms of our relationship with God. Consider the key issue of community. Any number of personal and social questions and situations are manifestations of the issue of community: the growing disparity between the rich and the poor; violence in the home, on the street, and among nations; the breakdown of the family; relationships among the races and between the genders; and the distance between the first and the third worlds. Can we learn to live together and with the environment in such a way that the future will be worth living? At bottom is our relationship with

God. Are we personally and corporately secure enough in God to put aside our self-created, false, manipulative, and oppressive securities standing in the way of a just and lasting community?

Of course, the pastor will want to give interpretive attention to things that are happening in culture and community. In 1986, when the space shuttle Challenger exploded with seven people on board, all kinds of questions were raised—from God's relationship with tragedy to the value of the space program in a world where the dichotomy between the rich and the poor grows ever wider. Such events rightly claim our homiletical attention.

The pastor will find it illuminating to watch the television news, read the newspapers, magazines (especially the advertisements), and contemporary novels, and to pay attention to contemporary artistic expression with a question in the back of the mind: "What does this tell me about the concerns of people today?"[31]

Some ministers have found it helpful to conduct surveys to give the congregation an opportunity to voice topics and texts that it would like to hear addressed in sermons. This procedure provides the preacher with a wonderful entrée to ask the congregation to view everything from effective parenting to the charismatic movement from the perspective of our relationship with God.

Many pastors also find it illuminating to organize a "sermon preparation group." The group, composed of the pastor and perceptive laity, meets early in the week. The pastor introduces the biblical text(s) and the subject of the sermon. The people respond to the text and the subject out of their own experience and concerns. From the conversation, the pastor gets a sense of when and where live connection is being made between the developing sermon and the people.

Another widely used group-centered model is the pastoral study group. Pastors conveniently located to one another meet together weekly to talk over forthcoming sermons. This type of group works especially well when the members of the group are preaching from a commonly used lectionary. In addition to providing homiletical inspiration, the group can function as a clergy support system.

Pastoral calling, especially routine home and office visits, is a critical lifeline connecting the congregation to the pulpit. A sensitive listener will be able to discern concerns and issues vital to the congregation and to the larger community. Indeed, Leander Keck calls such activity "priestly listening" and says that it is as important to the preparation of the sermon as listening to the biblical text.[32]

Diagnostic Question

3. What is the fundamental life issue with which this sermon is concerned?

4. The Bible Has a Prominent Place in the Sermon

Biblical texts and themes will have a prominent place in Christian preaching. While it is possible to preach an authentic Christian sermon without reference to the Bible, there are good reasons for dealing regularly and seriously with the Bible in the sermon.[33]

By declaring the Bible to be its canon, the church has declared that the Bible is essential to its life. While debate continues about the precise place and authority of the Bible in the church, nearly all agree that the Bible contains the master story of God's relationship with the world.[34] At its best, preaching interprets that story so that the renewing power of the love of God can be spoken through it. The preacher does not preach the Bible per se, but preaches the good news of God which comes as a result of the encounter with the Bible. (Even the critically trained biblical interpreter can easily slip into bibliolatry.)

The Christian community has consistently found that it comes into a fresh, vital relationship with God when it gathers around the Bible, engages the Bible in the light of Christian tradition, keeps in touch with its own experience, and reasons its way to a sensible understanding of the text. When the preacher and the congregation gather around the Bible in this way on Sunday morning and are illuminated by the power of the Holy

Spirit, the sermon has the power to reveal the love and purposes of God to the community, bestow identity, and empower the community for mission in the world.

Further, in popular culture in the United States, many people associate serious religious discourse with the Bible. For many people, the use of the Bible is a mark that the speaker's thoughts about God, life, and religion can be taken seriously.[35] Ironically, in our time, despite this high accord given to the Bible, biblical illiteracy is widespread in the church and in the world.[36] To still other listeners, the Bible is a dusty antique piece whose significance must be demonstrated.

Thus, whenever the preacher uses the Bible, two rules are in order. (1) Take nothing for granted about the listeners' knowledge of the Bible. The preacher will increase communication if the congregation is given an informational hook on which to hang biblical references and allusions. (2) The place of the Bible in the sermon and in the lives of the listeners will be enhanced if the preacher makes the Bible interesting and alive.

Furthermore, the use of the Bible in preaching imposes upon the preacher the responsibility of interpreting the Bible carefully and critically. In addition to the disciplines of historical and literary criticism, the preacher needs to practice theological criticism—the interpretation of the text in the light of the gospel.

The preacher reads the Bible looking for the good news in the text. A good question to ask of every biblical text would be: what is the good news for the congregation in this text?[37] The negative correlate is that some texts contain bad news which needs to be corrected by the preacher. For example, passages in the Bible condone slavery, the oppression of women, and anti-Judaism. In order for the sermon to be appropriate to the gospel, it may be necessary for the preacher to say sensitively but straightforwardly, "This text (or some element in the text) is bad news."[38] A companion question to ask of every pericope is: Does this text contain any bad news?

Many preachers in the last quarter of the 20th century are finding that a lectionary provides a good framework within which to encounter the Bible and from which to base the Sunday sermon. The kind of lectionary which is in the most common use today is the *lectio selecta* in which the Bible readings (*lectio*) are selected (*selecta*) according to the way in which they fit into the main emphases of the seasons of the Christian year.[39] Three readings are appointed for each Sunday: one from a gospel (which is the leading text for the day), one from another of the remaining twenty-six books from the canonical literature from the early church, and one from the Hebrew Bible. Some lectionaries also appoint a Psalm.

Preaching from the lectionary quite rightly is highly praised today.[40] The scriptures are interpreted within the theological framework of the drama of redemption as set forth by the Christian year. A wide range of passages is brought before the community, including many texts requiring serious theological wrestling that might otherwise be avoided; the lectionary makes it difficult for preachers continually to ride their "hobby horses." The Hebrew scriptures are given at least some public recognition. The annual pattern of readings helps shape the congregation's perception of God's presence and activity in the world.

Yet, the lectionaries of today also have limitations.[41] Truly selective, they reflect the social bias of their largely white, middle class designers by downplaying many of the texts emphasizing God's liberating activity on behalf of the poor and oppressed. For all the praise heaped upon them for making preacher and congregation wrestle with difficult texts, they slight some of the most difficult texts of all. For instance, that part of John 8 in which the Johannine Jesus accuses the Jews of being children of the devil is omitted altogether from the Common Lectionary. This causes the preacher to lose a significant moment for instruction on the interpretation of the text in the light of the gospel. Further, the Hebrew Bible is relegated to a supporting role in most lectionaries. The Hebrew Bible is four times the size of the canonical writings from the early church, and yet selections from the Hebrew Bible comprise only one-third of the readings in the lectionary. Even more damaging, the Hebrew readings often are interpreted as "prophecies," "fulfilled" only in the life of the church. Seldom are the readings from the Hebrew Bible allowed to stand on their own; they usually are heard in the light of the reading from the gospel, a reading that is frequently anti-Jewish in tone! This reinforces the notion that Judaism is a second-rate religion. And the thematic connection among the three readings for a given day is often quite artificial, thus creating a false sense of the "unity" of scripture.

Another kind of lectionary in use today, chiefly in evangelical circles, is the *lectio continua*. Week by week, the congregation reads continuously through a given book of the Bible. The continuous reading allows the congregation to enter into the world of the text and to follow its drama from beginning to end. One comes systematically to know a document and its strengths and weaknesses. This pattern is especially useful as the basis for preaching from the Hebrew Bible, a part of the canon which is neglected in the churches today.

Members of mainline congregations should be encouraged to bring their Bibles with them to church. Their knowledge of the Bible and its interpretation will be enhanced if they see passages as well as hear them. If the listeners had copies of the text before them, the pastor could engage in more detailed examination of the text in the course of the sermon and ask the congregation to examine other passages which illumine or challenge the primary passage for the day. With the text before them, the congregation will be stirred to engage in reflection on the passage and on the Christian life, and to ask its own questions of the text. The presence of Bibles would be particularly useful when the pastor is preaching against the text or when the preacher is drawing from a text a point which runs against the common assumptions of the congregation. Indeed, some members will be moved to join the adult Christian education program of the church.

Pew Bibles could be provided for those who do not bring their own copies from home, but they are not a substitute for members' own Bibles in hand. We learn the peculiarities of a house by living in it. We learn the Bible as we become accustomed not only to the words but to the print, to the way the text lies on the page, to the place in which the materials are found. Of course, such familiarity can have the effect of taming the text, but, more importantly, it can make one's copy of the Bible a wonderful resource for theological reflection and devotion. Only as the stories of the Bible become a part of our being and identity can we take our place in their continuation.

Diagnostic Question

4. Does the Bible appear in a prominent and appropriate place in this sermon?

25

5. The Preacher Speaks with Authority

Writing on the necessity of clear, intelligible speech in worship, the apostle Paul says, "If the trumpet gives an uncertain sound, who will prepare . . . to the battle?" (1 Corinthians 14:8, KJV). To draft this image into the service of preaching, the purpose of the sermon is to give the certain sound of the gospel in a most uncertain world.

Certainty in preaching is especially important today because of two characteristics of the world: pluralism and relativism. Many ideas, groups, and movements exist side by side in the world today, each offering good things to those who follow in its way and each competing with the others for loyalty. At the same time, there is no single, commonly accepted external authority by which one movement can be judged as "true" and other movements as "false." Devotees of Eastern gurus, fundamentalists, peddlers of self-help books, and representatives of the movement for a nuclear freeze-all stand on the same street corner at the same time, promising guidance and even salvation to people who desperately seek a reliable way forward. An uncertain sound will never be heard above the racket of the loudspeakers on the street corner.[42]

On matters of authority, until not long ago, the preacher could appeal to the Bible, tradition, or ordination.[43] These sources of authority were external to the sermon itself and could be invoked in order to justify a preacher's statements. But in today's pluralistic and relativistic world, listeners no longer simply assume the validity of these sources. It is not obvious to all that there is a God, much less that this God makes a real and positive difference to the world. To a world whose biggest selling drug is a painkiller, the promise of redemption through suffering love is strange indeed. Why should I die to myself when, by attending a few weekend seminars, I can learn how to get everything I ever wanted?

26

As William Baird says,

Some of the issues we face in congregations, and regional and general assemblies, require us to speak where the Bible seems to have nothing to say. At the same time, the Bible appears to speak about a lot of things (for instance, eating meat offered to idols) which don't concern us at all.[44]

Much the same is true of Christian tradition.

Furthermore, in daily life, the church no longer assumes many things presupposed in the world of the Bible. For instance, the validity of slavery is generally assumed in the Bible. In fact, the Bible nowhere prohibits slavery. But today we believe that slavery is immoral. Few in the church today would take 1 Peter 2:13 as valid in every time and place. "Be subject for the Lord's sake to every human institution, whether it be to the emperor as supreme or to governors sent by him. . . ." By this standard, the Nazis who murdered six million Jews during the Holocaust simply acted out the divinely prescribed responsibility to obey their leader, and the revolution of 1776, bringing the United States into being, showed flagrant disobedience to God. Thus, in order to blow a trumpet whose sound is certain and believable, the preacher must do more than blow harder.

The authority of the sermon can no longer rest only upon external sources commonly acknowledged by people today. In the contemporary climate, the preacher needs to develop internal authority, that is, evidence within the message itself for the listener to take seriously the claims of the sermon. The preacher may, therefore, want to engage in a modern version of apologetics (giving reasons why the claims of the gospel are persuasive in the modern world).[45] At this point, a helpful theological method and the preferences of listeners come together to help the preacher know how to speak with an authority that is soundly based and that will be recognized as authoritative by listeners.

Whether explicitly or implicitly, most church bodies today come to authoritative voice on beliefs, position on issues, lifestyles, and actions through careful consideration of four sources: the Bible, tradition of the church, experience of the community, and reason. Each of these sources makes a witness as to what is true, and therefore, is authoritative. The community listens to these witnesses, and, under the illumination of the Holy Spirit, judges what is authoritative for its life. The interaction of these sources may be diagrammed as follows.

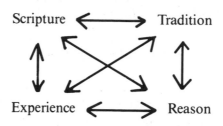

Scripture ←——→ Tradition

Experience ←——→ Reason

The testimony of each witness is validated, called into question, or modified by the other witnesses.[46]

Of special interest to us now are the roles of experience and reason in concluding what is authoritative. The experience of the community in both the inner life of its members and in its social interaction is a subjective proving ground for the message of the preacher. For instance, the sermon may promise that persons receive new life through baptism into Christ. The community will naturally ask, "Does that promise come true in the experience of those who are baptized? Do they find new life?" The preacher may claim that in the community of the baptized, distinctions of race, class, and gender lose their power. As Paul said in Galatians 3:27-28, "For as many of you as were baptized into Christ have put on Christ. There is neither Jew nor Greek . . . neither slave nor free . . . neither male nor female; for you all are one in Christ Jesus." When this is true in the social experience of the church, then the claim of the preacher is verified. The claim has behind it the authority of experience.

Reason compels us to ask if a given belief makes sense in the light of the way in which we think about the world today, especially the scientific world view. A community that asks its members to believe something about God and God's activity in the world that is incredible in the light of the modern view of the cosmos and its operation is in danger of losing its authority.

Reason also asks whether a given belief or action is consistent with other beliefs or actions held by the community and pro-

28

claimed from its pulpit. When a community says one thing but acts in a way contradictory to what it says, or when it says two things which contradict each other, the community's pronouncement can hardly be seen as authoritative. What, after all, does the community really believe?

A study of listeners has found that these two things—experience and reason—are highly persuasive. Most listeners want to be challenged to think. They want to understand. They want to know the reasoning for the positions they are being asked to adopt. And again, they want demonstration that the claims of the preacher are true. Of particular persuasiveness to the listener is the "evidential experience," the experience from real life illustrating the claim of the sermon. If the preacher promises renewed life because of the gospel, it is important to give an example of renewed life.[47]

In addition to the content of the message itself, two more items contribute to the authority of the sermon. The first is the conviction of the preacher. If the people sense that the sermon is a matter of real importance to the preacher, they are likely to take it seriously. People respond positively to appropriate and heart-felt passion. If, on the other hand, the preacher seems cool, distant, and detached, many listeners are likely to think that the subject is not very important to the preacher, and, therefore, need not be taken too seriously.[48]

The second is a sense of respect and trust for the preacher. As long ago as Aristotle's time[49] and as recently as the listener study to which reference has just been made,[50] the character of the speaker has been recognized as an important part of the authority of the speaker. Of particular significance is continuity between what is said and the life of the preacher. If the preacher consistently stresses love in sermons but treats people as if they are means to an end, the effect of the message is undermined. In this respect, one of the most effective ways to build trust in the pulpit is to engage in regular pastoral care and calling. Regularly opening the door to the nursing home creates its own authority.

Diagnostic Question

5. What, in this sermon, is an authoritative word for our time? Why could it be regarded as having authority?

6. Preaching Communicates the Offer of Salvation

Christian preaching will interpret the meaning of salvation for the modern world and communicate God's offer of salvation to the world.[51] In modes of thought, language, and imagery appropriate to the gospel and to our time, the preacher will describe salvation and place God's gracious offer before the congregation. This is important for two reasons.

First, salvation is the fundamental purpose of God for all of creation.[52] When we accept God's gracious offer, our perception of the character of existence changes. Once, we served false gods, were enslaved by sin, and suffered hopelessly from the brokenness of life. Now, because of grace, we serve the one living God, are freed from bondage to sin, and live purposefully even in the midst of brokenness. In language taken from the Bible and Christian tradition, salvation means the difference between death and life. If salvation is the purpose of God, and if the stakes are life and death, it follows that it is the church's business to communicate the offer of salvation to the world.

Secondly, salvation is a crucial matter for our time. Daily, signs of impending doom stalk us: the mounting world debt, environmental abuse, prolonged injustice that threatens to be ended by violence, terrorism, false values eating away like cancer at the heart of our culture, narcissism, escapism, and over it all, the shadow of the mushroom cloud. No wonder, like the rich ruler, many in our culture are asking, in individual and collective terms, "What must we do to be saved?" When the congregation comes to worship, it brings with it "the yearning for deliverance."[53]

Unfortunately, this yearning is often not met in the Sunday service. As Keith Watkins puts it,

> In Disciples churches, the message of salvation is strangely muted, even in the communion service that represents Christ's death for our sins. We seem to have forgotten the central fact of the gospel and the foundation of our life together in the church.[54]

30

This silence fails both to honor God (who in love wills to save the world) and to address the expressed concern of parishioners.

Every sermon cannot deal with salvation in a full way. But the subject of salvation can become a regular part of the preaching schedule. Nearly all sermons can point to some dimension of what it means to be saved and invite hearers to respond to the gospel with faith. And, of course, increased attention weekly to the salvific motifs of the Lord's Supper will dramatize and mediate the central meaning of the death and resurrection of Christ.

The turning to God to embrace the offer of salvation is at the same time a turning away from the false gods, false values, and evil practices of the world. The preaching of salvation thus becomes a dynamic context by which to call the congregation away from such things as idolatry, participation in injustice, and environmental abuse. Why continue to live in Babylon, the city of the great whore, the smoke of whose funeral pyre is already rising, when one can live in the new Jerusalem, drink from the water of life, and behold the unfading glory of God?

Diagnostic Question

6. How does this sermon communicate the offer of salvation?

7. The Sermon Is Clear

The sermon needs to be clear. In order for the congregation to receive and to respond to the good news, members need to be able to understand it. To put the issue crudely, the congregation needs to "get the point."

While this may seem self-evident, I know from experience that it is possible to sit through a sermon by an informed, intelligent, theologically alert, and ethically responsible preacher, and yet to leave the sanctuary as if emerging from a fog. The problem often seems to be lack of focus and discipline in the preparation of the sermon. The preacher has tried to say too much, too little, has not settled precisely upon what to say, or has not been able to communicate the idea. Occasionally I have even heard a sermon whose organizing principle is "stream of consciousness." From

31

sermon to sermon, and even within the same sermon, ideas can be in opposition to one another, thus leaving the hearer in a state of confusion. "Just what can I believe?"

Such homiletical events (or non events, as the case may be) do violence in several ways. If the messengers of God are incoherent and inconsistent, the listener may quietly begin to think that God is incoherent and inconsistent. The preacher may call into question his or her competence as an interpreter of the Christian faith and thus erode the relationship of trust between pulpit and pew. Being frustrated week after week, the listeners may tune out.

But it need not be so. The sermon can bring the congregation into the presence of large and promising realities. These can deeply affect the congregation. This happens as the preacher becomes clear about the purpose of a particular sermon.

One of the most honored axioms of preaching states that the thrust of the sermon should be expressed in one sentence. This sentence is called by different names, i.e., "the proposition," "thesis statement," "big idea," or "the sermon in a sentence." Whatever it is called, the preparation of the sermon will be greatly helped by the writing of such a sentence. The sermon then becomes that sentence "written large."

This sentence is best when it is a simple sentence:

Subject / Verb / Predicate

The simpler the sentence, the better. The more complicated this sentence becomes, the more complicated the sermon becomes. The sentence will ordinarily be in the indicative mood (rather than the imperative mood). That is, the sentence will state what is, especially what God is doing (or what God has already done) much more often than it will command the congregation to do something. (See No. 8, page 35.) The character of the good news will be honored and the receptivity of the listeners increased if the sentence is stated *positively*.

Further, since the purpose of the sermon is to bring good news from God about life, this sentence is strengthened if it directly mentions God and the specific good news from God to be communicated in the sermon. Most of the time, God is the subject of the sentence and the verb is an action of God.

Closely related to the sermon in a sentence, but different, is the matter of what the sermon is intended to accomplish. If the subject of the sermon is forgiveness, the preacher may want the congregation to feel forgiven. If the sermon is on the trustworthiness of God, the result of the sermon may be for the listeners to trust in God. A convenient way to get at what the sermon is to accomplish is to ask the question, "What do I want this sermon to accomplish in the lives of the listeners?"

Before developing the sermon, the preacher may want to consider whether or not the major idea of the sermon is really worth preaching. Is it large enough and important enough to become the focus for the only time during the week when the whole congregation will think together about essential matters of the Christian faith?

The sermon in a sentence becomes a magnet, attracting all manner of illuminating material from the course of pastoral ministry: an item in the newspaper, a parishioner's comment, an experience in the hospital, a report from a government agency, a paragraph from a novel, an intuition that comes through prayer. The sermon in a sentence also becomes a machete by which the preacher can trim away all interesting but unrelated material.

One occasionally hears that a sermon is "too intellectual." This usually means that the sermon is obscure, pedantic, dull, and without apparent significance to the hearer. At the least, it indicates that the preacher has not taken full account of his or her responsibility to make the point of the sermon clear.

Once the sermon in a sentence is formulated, the preparation of the sermon proper begins with decisions about form and structure. If one is working with a traditional, deductive structure, it will be fairly easy to get "the point" in the sermon painted in unmistakable colors. If one is developing the sermon along the lines of the newer, more indirect approaches, such as "inductive preaching"[55] or "sermon as story,"[56] the task will be much more difficult. In the latter cases, the homiletical responsibility is compounded. To the question of "What will the sermon say?" is added the question of "How will the sermon say it?"

Diagnostic Question

7. Put the sermon into a simple, indicative sentence. What do you hope this sermon will accomplish in the lives of the listeners?

8. Christian Preaching Is Basically Indicative

One of the most theologically helpful things we learn in the study of verbs in high school English is the difference between the indicative and the imperative. Verbs which are in the indicative mood describe the way things are. For example, "God loves you." The imperative is the mood of command. "Love your neighbor."

By nature, the gospel first of all is indicative. It is the announcement of God's love for the world. That is the way things are, and it is the preacher's blessed work to make it known. The gospel, then, first is good news. Instruction follows.

However, much contemporary Christian preaching is dominated by the imperative. In its worst form, the sermon is reduced to moralizing. "Moralizing sermons invariably emphasize things to be done, virtues to be developed or even beliefs to be held."[57] Jesus becomes an example whom we are to imitate rather than one through whom God gives us life and power. The preacher frequently tells the people to be good or to do good: "Witness for peace," "hire a woman," "boycott the products of a multinational corporation."

The imperative assumes that people know who they are, why they should respond, and that they are filled with the spiritual power to carry out the command. In other words, the imperative assumes that the congregation has heard and welcomed the indicative. But the congregation's acceptance can no longer be taken for granted in mainline Protestant churches. Because of such factors as the cultural captivity of the church, the loss of familiarity with the Bible, the decline of attendance at Sunday school and other places where regular instruction in the Christian faith is given, and a generation (or more) of moralizing from the pulpit, the modern church is malnourished. Some of our churches are little more than optimistic clubs with a cross on the wall. (Or some may be less than optimistic clubs.)

In our situation, when the imperative is spoken without the indicative, it lacks the power to achieve the very thing it commands. In fact, it ultimately works against itself. The people feel the weight of the command, but they lack the power to carry it out, and are left with a burden of guilt. The imperative creates the very conditions that require good news! Furthermore, the imperative not only is impotent to save, it leaves the congregation feeling as though God is an old nag whose cosmic pleasure is getting on people's backs. Those few who obey the command may well take false security, supposing that in their obedience they have put God in their debt.

Of course, the indicative itself can be preached in a distorted way. The congregation can easily become ingrown, thinking that its only purpose in the world is to lie under the sunlamp of the gospel.

The preacher's responsibility is to place the indicative and the imperative in proper relationship in the local setting. The ideal situation is for the congregation to be built up in the gospel in such a way that they will ask, "What, then, shall we do?"

Thus it is imperative (!) that the stress of the sermon fall regularly on the indicative. The importance of regular indicative preaching is indicated by the regularity of worship itself. In only seven days we can begin to forget who we are and why we are in the world. Preaching in which the indicative and the imperative are in healthy relationship can contribute much to the congregation awakening on Sunday morning with expectation and enthusiasm. "Ah! The best day of the week!" And so it is when we learn who we are and what we are to do.

Diagnostic Question

8. What is the evidence that this sermon is basically indicative?

9. The Preacher Speaks from Person to Person

The effectiveness of preaching is increased when it is clearly a word spoken from person to person. Preaching is "first, last, and all the time a function of the personal world."[58] To use a phrase made familiar by Martin Buber, preaching is an "I-Thou" relationship between two selves.[59] To be sure, this relationship is complicated in preaching by the preacher's usual format. The preacher stands in monologue before a large number of people. Nonetheless, even in a sanctuary filled with several hundred worshipers, the act of preaching can be a lively encounter in which person speaks to person. The sermon, which is monologue in form, can become dialogical in feeling.[60]

Two considerations point to the importance of preaching having this quality. First, as long ago as the Hebrew Bible, at the heart of the Jewish and Christian tradition(s), God is confessed to be a "Thou." The Gospel of John even sees Jesus as "The Word become flesh." The doctrine of the incarnation is at least partly an attempt to say that in Jesus Christ we encounter God as a "Thou." While the nature of God's being and "personhood" continue to be discussed,[61] it is never enough for a Christian to see God as Emily Dickinson's "hazy, oblong blur." Therefore, in order to be consistent with the nature of God, the sermon is a word from an "I to a Thou." If the relationship between preacher and hearer becomes a relationship of "I-It," the hearer may project the quality of "itness" onto God.

Further, to speak to the listener as a person is to communicate at a basic and fundamental human level not often touched in our "high-tech" world. In this world an increasing amount of communication takes place through technological systems: (e.g., print, radio, tape recordings, television, computers, automated bank tellers, undisguised computer-generated letters). In this setting it is easy for people to feel passive, nonvalued, even alien.

While making a pastoral call one afternoon, I was taken aback by a conversation with a senior member of our congregation who lived alone in a high-rise apartment not far from the church building. She said she got up in the morning and ate by herself in total silence. The first voice she heard in the day was on the radio. When she went to the store, she was a check. When she went to the Social Security office, she was a problem. When she went to the dentist, she was a cavity. When she went to the church choir, she was a voice. To such people, the sermon can come as a welcome human word.

The spectacular productions of the media have eroded the confidence of some ministers in the capacity of the sermon and the service of worship to hold the attention of the modern listener. "How can I compete with Michael Jackson, Rambo, or Robert Schuller?" While the media has affected modern people (e.g., conditioning the average television viewer to focus attention for just seven to ten minutes at a time), the media cannot replace the living encounter of person to person. The modern church will only be distracted and ultimately embarrassed if it tries to make Sunday morning a sacred version of "The Price Is Right." The need is not for more show biz but for a meaningful word from the Lord in a genuine human encounter.

The most important signal to the congregation that the preacher is speaking as an "I-Thou" is the preacher's attitude, not only during the sermon but in the course of daily ministry.[62] Beyond this, four clues can help establish and maintain the personal quality of preaching.

First is the use of the pronouns "I" and "you." The "I" is important because it identifies the preacher as a specific person responsible for the content of the message. More important is the use of "you." For this is the language of direct address and when rightly used, puts the matter of the sermon clearly before the listener. "Well, what do *you* think?"

Most of the time, preachers should avoid generic terms like "one" (in reference to a person), "humankind," or "people." These terms, and their cousins, will not usually get under the skin of the listener. Consider the difference between these two statements:

> God speaks to humankind.
> God speaks to you.

Further, H. H. Farmer finds ineffective the use of the homiletical "we."

We feel this, the preacher says, we ought to do that, we naturally ask such and such a question. The result is that *we* get the impression that we are just sitting back and talking *about* God, whereas in effective preaching, *you*, my friend, would be inescapably aware that God is talking to *you*, asking *you* questions which you must answer, offering *you* here and now the succor which *you* most desperately need.[63]

Further, the homiletical "we" can be reminiscent of a parent talking to a small child, "We don't do that."[64]

Second, the human quality of preaching is increased when the preacher identifies with the congregation and stands with them in need of grace. The preacher is clearly not above the congregation, but in solidarity with them. This is also theologically correct.

Third, the judicious and appropriate use of the preacher's life experience can give the sermon a personal quality.[65] On the one hand, it is particularly good for the preacher to describe his or her struggle with an issue, problem, or situation.[66] The congregation identifies with the struggle and finds a benediction for its own struggles. On the other hand, the effect is reversed when the preacher turns out to be the hero or heroine. That creates a sense of distance from the congregation. The personal experience of the preacher comes into the sermon only as a living lens for the gospel and is always governed by a sense of good taste and appropriateness.

Fourth, direct reference to the community in which the sermon is given and to the affairs that affect the daily lives of the congregation is a clear signal of personal concern.[67] References to the local community indicate that the preacher has been paying careful attention to the daily world of the congregation. The listeners think, "We are important!" This attention, after all, is fundamental to good news. If the preacher pays attention to the child hit by the car, then surely God does so as well.

Diagnostic Question

9. In this sermon, what are the signals that it is addressed from person to person?

10. The Sermon Helps the Congregation Make a Choice

While the gospel is proclaimed to all, it is not forced upon any. Each person is free to accept or to reject the good news, either in general or in its specific manifestation in a sermon. The preacher will be of service both to the gospel and the congregation by putting members of the congregation in the position of making a choice, a decision, about the gospel and the major thrust of the sermon. Do I accept God's gracious offer and live in its grace and freedom, or do I turn away and cling to the broken but familiar and secure? Only when we choose are we fully available to that which we have chosen.[68]

In our setting, several factors hinder people from realizing that they need to make such a choice. In the mainline churches, new members are often the result of "biological growth." The children of members are shuttled through baptism (or confirmation), but never really choose between the gods of our culture and the God of Abraham and Sarah. When they grow up, they move away and transfer their membership into a new congregation. Soon they turn up serving in the diaconate and later being ordained elders. But they may never really choose the gospel.

At the popular level in the United States, the values and practices of the culture are often identified with the values and practices of the Christian faith. One can drift into (and out of) the church without having one's perspective on life fundamentally altered. Of course, this is partly because we in the church have preached the highest values of our culture as the gospel: morality, kindness, honesty, progress, growth, hard work, and goodness. In a community where my spouse and I once served, a leading congregation was known as "the country club on its knees at prayer." It not always is obvious that an essential choice needs to be made.

Unbelievers who come into contact for the first time with this kind of religion ask, "What difference does it make?" Already moral, living useful lives in the world (some of them in real human service), they see no need to turn to God.

For still others, the gospel is a kind of additive to life. Like putting STP in the gas tank of the car, the gospel makes life run a little smoother and with fewer knocks. In the pulpits of the crass, to accept the gospel is to get on God's payroll, the benefits of which include things like health, beauty, a job, and money. This simply is materialism, baptized in the name of God.

In such a setting, the preacher does the congregation no better service than clarifying the choice between serving Mammon and serving the living God. Otherwise, the community is not only deprived of genuine blessing, but is living on the basis of false premises.

There is no single "prime grade" homiletic to put people in the position of making a choice. It can be done quite directly. For example, "Given the difference between God and the gods beyond the river, 'Choose this day whom you will serve.'" While such direct, frontal assaults will be clarifying for some, they will prove too harsh for others. These others will become defensive and retreat into thick-walled bunkers of resistance.

The question can be put to the congregation more indirectly. For instance, Fred Craddock proposes to let the listener "overhear" the gospel.[69] The sermon puts the listener in the position of over-hearing a conversation about substantial matters. With resistance lowered, the listener is more receptive to these matters and makes a decision about them. There is no substitute here for the preacher's own sensitivity and imagination.

The imperative is to be used cautiously. "Many churchgoers have been led to expect a dreary procession of musts, oughts, and shoulds which bounce off their hides like hailstones off concrete."[70]

Diagnostic Question

10. How does this sermon help the listener come to a decision about the gospel?

11. Preaching Is Concrete

Concreteness is a consistent mark of effective Christian preaching. When the gospel is expressed in concrete, specific terms and is concretely related to the situation of the listeners, the listeners are better able to feel the sermon addressed to them.[71] Through the use of the concrete, the gospel gets under the skin of the listeners, "piercing to the division of soul and spirit, of joints and marrow, and discerning the thoughts and intentions of the heart" (Hebrews 4:12).

At base, this is a theological concern. God relates to specific people, specific situations, even specific worlds, in specific ways. While it is true that God loves not only all people but all of creation, we best understand that love when we see it expressed in particular situations and then use those situations as a lens through which to see the gospel in Judea and Samaria and in all the ends of the earth. For instance, God did not simply "love" the people of Israel, but called Abraham and Sarah, delivered the Israelite slaves from Egypt, raised Jesus from the dead. The seminal events of our tradition are specific and concrete. Because they are paradigmatic, through them we see how the presence, purpose, and power of God are revealed in the particular and discrete.[72]

Concreteness, of course, is in contrast to abstraction and generalization. Preachers have several tendencies that result in over-populating the sermon with abstractions and generalities. For one, many of the central words and concepts of our faith have come down to us as abstractions. (e.g., faith, salvation, justification.) Yet, these nouns have often become dull and dim from age and overuse, and they shift the focus of attention from the primary and specific to the secondary and general. For another, it is easier to use handy and prepackaged abstractions than to develop fresh concrete expressions and images. Again, we sometimes think that by making a generalization, a message will have wider application.

In fact, hidden behind the abstract nouns of our tradition, we often find action verbs. The abstract noun is a shorthand expression of the action and its result. Not only are the actions themselves more picturesque, but they identify God as one who (in the problematic expression) acts. The hearer, therefore, begins to think that God may continue to act in the world.

Ironically, generalizations often have the effect of blunting a specific, driving point. For a statement that is made about everyone to anyone can easily be construed as a statement meant for no one. When a specific image is used, the listener is able to see his or her experience refracted through the specific image. Therefore, "Preachers will learn to ask themselves, when tempted to use a generalization, 'What specifically do you have in mind?'"[73]

According to David Buttrick, the preacher stands between the old images and expressions of the Christian faith and the community. Taking the images, metaphors, and symbols of the tradition (nearly all of which are quite concrete), the preacher tries to give them newer, concrete expression. In this sense, the preacher is a "reverse theologian," whose calling is to re-image the Christian faith in ways that make it alive and meaningful to the contemporary congregation.[74]

To put it negatively, if the pastor is not ready to illustrate a point, to give it flesh and blood, she or he is not ready to preach that point. If one is speaking about "love," the natural question will be, "Where is a picture of love?" If one is speaking about joy, a natural question will be, "What can I do in the sermon to help the congregation feel joyous?"

Concrete images can be suggested by as many situations as there are in life: seeing an artist's poignant painting, stumbling barefoot through the dark, comforting a crying child, stepping on a Lego. The gospel and concrete situations can be brought together.

Particularly useful, in my judgment, is material from the life of the community in which the sermon is being preached. When used with care and discretion, local imagery has three values: (1) The people know that the pastor has taken them seriously; (2) the gospel is related directly to the situation of the congregation; (3) their trust in the gospel is increased as they see it applied to situations they know: "Well, that's old Joe who sits in the cane bottom rocker on the square and spits his tobacco juice on the ground. If it can happen to him, maybe it can happen to me." Of course, this prescription needs to be kept in tension with the need to see the gospel addressed to larger social settings and the need to enlarge the horizon of the congregation through the use of concrete material from other settings and cultures. But whatever the source and purpose of an image, the need for concreteness remains the same.

No sermon is ready to preach until it contains at least one real-life image that embodies the thrust of the sermon. With apologies for using the doctrine of the incarnation, only then does the word of the sermon become flesh.

Diagnostic Question

11. What are the concrete elements in this sermon?

12. Humor Can Serve the Gospel

While certainly not a requirement for Christian preaching, the appropriate use of humor often can help a theologically adequate but otherwise lame sermon to rise up and walk. Humor, of course, is never used for its own sake. Like everything else in the sermon, it serves the gospel and the major point of the sermon. Humor has several qualities that commend its use in the sermon.

At the simplest level, it helps hold the attention of the hearers. In these deadly serious times, laughter also breaks the tension of life and gives us a sense of relief, even if only for a few minutes. Without wanting to stretch the point too far, a humorous moment communicates something of what happens when the gospel breaks into human life: the binding grip of sin and death is broken, and we are free to rejoice in God, in one another, and in the world.[73] Indeed, in this sense, laughter has an eschatological character.[76] For Frederick Buechner, the gospel itself has a comic character precisely because it is unexpected. In a world of sorrow and tragedy, who would expect that the maker of heaven and earth would cause a ninety-year-old woman to become pregnant, or raise a crucified criminal from the dead, or justify you and me?[77]

Like soil stiffening all winter but broken up by the spade in spring, humor loosens up the congregation. By putting listeners in a relaxed frame of mind, their defenses are lowered, and they become more receptive to the message of the sermon.

In the hands of the skillful and careful preacher, humor can also be used to expose who we are. Writing about the necessity of reading the Bible with honest humor, James A. Sanders gives an example that is applicable to preaching. "We have to smile a bit when we see ourselves in Abraham fall prostrate before the deity in a posture of great piety, and instead of praying, see him (find ourselves) snickering at the thought that God can do the impossible (Genesis 18:14; Luke 1:37), especially without our help."[78] Through such humor, we come to see our need of grace.

Great care needs to be taken by the preacher who uses humor. David Buttrick cautions that it is important for the preacher to know why (and when) he or she wants the congregation to laugh.[79] Otherwise, the humor may simply be distracting. Also it is important not to make laughter at the expense of the dignity of others or to use humor to justify (or make easier) inappropriate behavior and attitudes.

The canned joke is usually less than satisfactory in sermons. Seldom do such jokes "make the point" and seldom do they ring true to the living experience of the listener. They even sound second-hand and second-rate. The difference between a canned joke and living humor is like the difference between striking a teaspoon first against a juice-sized glass that formerly held jelly and then against a crystal goblet.

The best humor is that which the pastor finds in the incongruities and surprises in the biblical text, in the life of the congregation, in events near and far. By finding humor in such places, the preacher may help the people find God there, too.

Diagnostic Question

12. How does the humor in this sermon serve the major point?

13. Graphic Speech Stimulates the Listener

A positive evaluation is nearly always given to a sermon judiciously sprinkled with graphic figures of speech and vivid metaphors.[80] Sense images, in particular, give the listener something to see, hear, touch, taste, and smell. The graphic elements can be as brief as appropriately chosen adjectives or as long as a fully developed narrative. Whether using a single word or several paragraphs, the preacher paints pictures in the minds of the listeners.

At the simplest level, graphic imagery makes the sermon interesting and colorful. Not only is the sermon interesting to the hearer, but the sermon can become especially memorable and, thus, can easily be carried from the service into the week.

On another level, graphic speech stimulates the minds and imaginations of the listeners so that they become more actively involved in the sermon than when the sermon contains only conceptual language.[81]

It follows that the more deeply involved the listener becomes in the sermon, the more deeply the gospel is able to penetrate the life of that listener. Indeed, when language is used carefully and intentionally, it can paint a new world for the listeners that they can enter via the imagination. Through the language and imagery of the sermon, the listener can experience the world shaped by the power of the gospel, and hence, be better able to choose the gospel.[82] The sermon posits a symbolic universe for the listener.[83]

Images help pattern the listener to recognize God's presence in the world. Indeed, one of the reasons for devoting a special hour of the week to worshiping and preaching is to be able to recognize the presence of God in every time and place. The hour of worship serves as a lens through which to interpret God's presence in all of life. The everyday world of the listener is filled with sensory images.[84] The listener who is accustomed to hearing the gospel interpreted in sensory images should better be able to recognize the presence of God in the everyday world.

Further, studies in the philosophy of language and in the psychology of consciousness conclude that sense images contribute to human understanding in important ways. Susanne K. Langer, for instance, has shown that human understanding takes place in two modes. One mode is discursive and informational. Speech often is basically informational. "God is love." "God loves you." The advantage of discursive speech is clarity and precision of expression. Powerful ideas can be expressed discursively.[85] The other mode of understanding is intuitive and emotive. Sensory data are simply presented to the self. They become a part of the intuitive knowledge of the self, even though they are not consciously analyzed by the mind. Works of art, such as paintings, dance, and music, are presented to the self through the appropriate senses.[86] Language has the remarkable capacity to be both discursive and presentational. Thus, through a logical and persuasive argument into which is woven provocative images, the preacher can speak discursively and presentationally at the same time. Thereby, the sermon speaks to the whole of the listener's understanding.

Research in the psychology of consciousness also has determined that the two halves of the brain control two different modes of knowledge. The left hemisphere of the brain is concerned with linear, rational thought. The right hemisphere is concerned with the intuitive, aesthetic, and imaginative. Sensory images speak especially to the right side of the brain. Fullness of understanding comes when both sides of the brain are engaged. Thus, preaching ideas that are strong and that appeal to the senses will address the full consciousness of the listener.[87]

The best images are suggested by life itself:

> From the time a baby reaches from the crib to catch the sunbeam streaming through a keyhole until the day when he sits old and alone among the pigeons in the park, the significant turns in the long road are marked by images with an emotional force that lingers in the memory long after the factual details are faded and dim. (Craddock)[88]

46

The preacher is open to such images in life and sensitively brings them into the sermon, being careful not to let their emotive power drift into shallow emotionalism.

A few guidelines can help the sermon become more graphic:

1. Keep sentences as simple as possible. The ear cannot follow long and complicated sentences.
2. Use active verbs. Passive constructions are not only ungainly, but communicate that both the preacher and God are passive.
3. Use adjectives that touch the five senses.
4. Ordinarily, use only one adjective at a time.
5. Avoid words with over three syllables.
6. Use everyday language and avoid words loaded with special religious meaning.
7. Explain religious vocabulary appearing in the sermon. *Propitiation*, for example, is no longer a household word. (One of the best ways to explain an unfamiliar word or concept is to paint a word-picture of it.)
8. When tempted to use an abstract noun, or even a concrete noun, consider using a verb construction instead. For instance, consider the differences in the following statements:

> —We have redemption from God.
> God redeems you and me.

9. Let preachers become as flypaper so that wherever they go, images stick to their minds: calling in the nursery at the hospital, marching in a protest against apartheid, watching a mother spider make a web.[89]

One illustration of a specific point at a time is normally sufficient in the sermon. More than one illustration may actually turn off the listener.[90]

A lean, well-developed narrative is especially forceful in preaching. As the congregation is drawn into the plot, they find their own lives in the story. Empathizing with characters and events helps them experience the story: its hope becomes their hope, its joy becomes their joy.[91] The experience of the narrative can become a redemptive event for the listener.

Hans van der Geest finds that in order for the hearers to identify fully with a narrative, the preacher needs to touch the "level of existential feelings, of expectation, disappointment, yearning, joy, sadness, and desire: only then do the people in the service hear their own story."[92] Yet, clearly for the listener as well as for the service of the gospel, the story is always a vehicle for proclamation. Whether or not religious words appear in the narrative or in the homiletical setting, its quality as a vehicle of religious truth needs to be clear to the listeners.[93] Therefore, the preacher needs not only to craft the story very carefully but to be very clear about the purpose of the narrative and how it will function in the sermon as a bearer of the good news.

In a sermon, the close companionship of powerful ideas, concreteness, graphic speech, and sensory images can move the listeners deeply and cause them to know why they are moved. At its best, preaching can evoke the experience of the gospel for the listener. Receiving the gospel at the fundamental level of human life, where rational decision and emotional power surge together, the listener is given the power to live out the gospel.

Before closing this section, two qualifications need to be made. One is that graphic speech can be overdone. The mind can only absorb a few images at a time. And the language can become so colorful and overbearing that it calls attention to itself. "Oh Brother Allen," she said, "I just love the way you use words." When the language gets in the way of the message, the preacher has traded display of her or his skills for communication of the gospel. Another is that listeners appreciate a balance of the graphic and the conceptual. The conceptual makes the meaning specific and unmistakable. "The preacher can expect the optimum effect only when there is a balance between graphic and conceptual speech."[94] To oversimplify: graphic speech excites the listener; conceptual speech interprets the excitement.

Diagnostic Exercise

13. With a red pencil, mark the elements of graphic speech in the sermon.

  a. In this sermon, what does the listener:
    (1) See?
    (2) Hear?
    (3) Touch?
    (4) Taste?
    (5) Smell?

b. How do the elements of graphic speech help the sermon achieve its purpose?
c. Does any of the graphic language in the sermon call attention to itself?
d. Where in the sermon could more graphic speech be used?

14. The Christian Sermon Is Inclusive

The matter of inclusivity has burst with force onto the religious scene in North America. While we often think first of the need for gender-inclusive language, the call for inclusivity extends far beyond finding new ways to talk about humankind and God. It includes those about whom we talk (as well as how we talk about them).

The fundamental affirmation of the gospel is that God loves all. Therefore, when the preacher uses illustrations and images that include "all," continuity is maintained between the gospel and the sermon. The subject matter of the sermon embodies the concern of God. If, on the other hand, the sermon continues to speak only of one type of person (or group) in its pronouns, references to God and humankind, subject matter, and illustrations, an implicit message is sent (even unintentionally) to those who are excluded: the preacher doesn't care about you, neither does the church and, perhaps, neither does God. Such exclusivity reinforces patterns of alienation, feeds distrust in God, and contributes to abuse of persons.

Of course, the preacher cannot speak to or about "all" people in sweeping generalizations. The principle of concreteness argues that the gospel is presented most powerfully when it is related to concrete situations. And the best images are specific. The preacher, therefore, will want to develop the self-consciousness to see that in the regular course of one's preaching, illustrations and images addressing the whole of the congregation are included in the sermons. Material will be selected that speaks of men, women, blacks, whites, Asian-Americans, Hispanics, the young, middle aged, old, white-collar power brokers, and still others who are broken by the ways in which the white collar types broker power.

By such inclusivity, the gospel is related concretely to the lives of the listeners, and the appeal and interest of the sermon is broadened. Incidentally, people do not respond only to sermonic material that includes their type. A white, upper middle-class "suburbanite" can be deeply moved by a story of an Ethiopian refugee. But when one of the listener's own kind appears in the sermon, it says in a simple and direct way, "The preacher takes me seriously."

To help the preacher develop a discipline for keeping track of the kinds of allusions, images, and illustrations usually appearing in sermons, I have developed a sample "inclusivity grid," included at the end of this section. In order for such a grid to be of maximum benefit in a local setting, the preacher will want to identify the constituent elements of the congregation (and the area in which the congregation is located) and include them on the grid. It is often revealing to use the grid for six or eight weeks, marking those categories that appear in the language and imagery of the sermon. The preacher can then begin to include those who are omitted.[95]

If the concrete references in sermons are limited to the constituency hearing the sermon, parochialism can result. Therefore, the preacher will want to use the allusions, imagery, and situations of the sermon to enlarge the congregation's awareness of the world and the ways in which God loves all.

With a minimum of self-conscious attention, language referring to humankind can gracefully be made inclusive.[96] Indeed, there is no reason at all to refer to humankind as "man" or "he." If the sermon takes the I-Thou relationship as its model, the preacher will typically speak in the language of "I" and "you." Thereby, many of the difficulties which beset inclusive writing will be avoided.

At times, of course, it will be necessary to speak in the third person. Keith Watkins points out that frequently the noun acting as the antecedent of the third person pronoun can be put into the plural so that its pronoun becomes the plural "they": "Preachers use inclusive language in their sermons." When it is necessary to use the third person singular pronoun, a phrase like "he or she" will slide off the tongue and into the ear as naturally as water into a glass.

Speaking about God in a sermon is more difficult because both the theological and grammatical complexities increase. All language about God is, by definition, metaphorical. The metaphors we use substantially shape our perception of God and our relationship with God. And the metaphors with which we speak of God have important personal and social implications. We can particularly thank perceptive women interpreters for taking the lead in showing that the continuous and dominant reference to God as "Father" serves to legitimate patriarchal culture that is oppressive to women. Indeed, in the western church, many of the ways by which we speak of God are masculine, and so, contribute to the subjugation of women.

Other metaphors for God contribute in other ways to human oppression. For example, to call God "Master" is to evoke the master-slave relationship and thereby imply that slavery is rooted in the divine order. The claim that God is light and one in whom there is no darkness at all has the social effect of downgrading people of color.[97]

What shall we do?[98] Patriarchy is so resilient that we may need to have a moratorium on gender-specific images for God for a generation. However, to remove all gender-specific references to God, thereby speaking of God only in the neuter, would also omit important qualities of our relationship with God. It may, therefore, be wise to search for the several descriptions of God from the Bible and Christian tradition that speak of God in feminine terms and as having feminine roles and to bring these alongside some traditionally masculine images into the common speech of the church. Even more, we can work in a conscientious way toward developing fresh language and imagery for God that is rooted in deep human experience and is faithful to the Christian tradition. We can speak of God in terms that capture the interplay of the various aspects of the inexhaustible being and activity of God, e.g., the intimate and the powerful, the awesome and the gentle. New and reclaimed metaphors can be used in preaching in quite natural ways that build up the church.

The practical difficulty for the speaker is the third person singular pronoun in reference to God. It will not do to refer to God as "it." To use "he" and "she" alternately is as confusing and jarring as a traffic light that changes from red to green every two seconds. One cannot substitute "God" every time a "he" would appear. Sentences would soon begin to sink beneath an overload of the word "God." Our reservoir of substitute terminology (e.g., "the divine being") is small and sometimes infelicitous. Keith Watkins may again point the way forward by suggesting that preachers rearrange sentences so that adjectives and epithets take the place of pronouns. In any case, the preacher will need to think carefully (and ahead of time!) about ways of speaking that avoid the awkward third person and make graceful amendments that are pleasing to the ear.[99]

Diagnostic Exercise

14. Using categories appropriate to the setting of the congregation in which the sermon was preached, create and mark an "inclusivity grid" like the following.

	Children	Youth	Young Adult	Middle Adult	Senior Adult
Men					
Women					
Blacks					
Whites					
Asian-Americans					
Hispanics					
Middle Class					
Lower Class					
Etc.					

15. The Sermon Is an Oral Event

For years, homiletics textbooks have emphasized that preachers should prepare sermons to be heard rather than to be read. In a memorable phrase, someone said that "the preacher aims for the ear." In recent years, careful study of the differences between oral and written expression has added impetus to this admonition. These are not only different modes of communication; they are also fundamentally different means of knowing (consciousness).[100] To "aim for the ear," then, is more than a matter of style.

Belden C. Lane points out four characteristics of oral consciousness.[101] First, sound is very much like "oral touch." When the speaker speaks and the listener listens, something physical actually happens in the ear of the listener. The ear itself is set in motion by the vibration of the soundwaves, giving speech a special force in the consciousness of the hearer.

> I've had the experience of missing a visual clue in a horror movie (not seeing the hand of the killer strike out, for example) but then finding myself frightened ever so much more by the screams in the audience around me—because the sound carried even more fear than the sight.[102]

The kinesthetic dimension of speaking and hearing gives the oral-aural transaction powerful immediacy in the mind and heart of the listener.

Second, the spoken word has a passing character. It is for the moment in which it is spoken, and after being spoken, it is gone. As a "living event," its life is shaped by the context in which it is spoken, and after that if the speaker sees that the listeners are not being touched by the speech, the speaker can adapt the content and manner of presentation. Through memory, of course, oral discourse can be kept alive, which often has a greater impact on its recipients than that of print.

Thirdly, oral speech has the quality of "bubbling spontaneity."

> From the lalling of infants to the experience of brain-storming sessions in a circle of friends, we are made aware of the copious flow that characterizes the spoken word . . . .

> We've all experienced intense conversations where exciting
> ideas were shared and we wanted so much to write things
> down, but were afraid to interrupt the magic, lest the act
> of writing should stop the flow.[103]

Oral speech has much more the character of give-and-take conversation than it does the character of reading a manuscript aloud. In oral culture, even memorized address has the quality of immediacy.

Fourth, oral speech is a communal event. It takes at least two persons in order to speak and to hear. And the act of speaking creates community, at least for the duration of the language event.[104]

What are some of the characteristics of oral speech?[105] Oral discourse typically reflects the context in which it is given. Later, remembrance of the ideas generated in that event will usually be tied to the event itself so that the later speaker would tell the story of the previous event and not simply abstract principles from it. Indeed, one finds stories and other concrete visual images permeating almost all of oral culture and almost no abstractions and generalities.

As aids to memory, oral discourse turns repeatedly to repetition and formulas, and to putting things into colorful, easily-recalled phrases. Indeed, purposeful repetition is a hallmark of oral discourse. The oral speaker frequently strings long sections together with the use of "and." "And Joseph . . . and . . . and . . . and . . . and." This looks peculiar in a printed manuscript, but it listens very well.

Epithets are used to strengthen images in the minds of the listener. Instead of saying "the oak," one might say, "the sturdy oak." Where the writer might use an analytical category to describe a person (e.g., the president is a menace), the speaker might tell a story showing the presidential menace.

Oral speech is not always given in neat paragraphs in which every sentence has a subject and a verb. In fact, true speech is filled with expletives, sentence fragments, and intonations, making all the difference in the world how a sentence is interpreted. In oral talk, one's voice can range all the way from the booming and the dramatic to the barest whisper.

Knowledge of orality is helpful to the preacher both in the preacher's thinking about the sermon and in the actual preparation and delivery of the sermon. Significantly, the preacher's confidence is increased that something really happens when the sermon is preached. Air waves really move. And more, as the folks in the New Hermeneutic used to say, preaching is a language *event* that has the power to effect the congregation deeply.

The preacher who is seeking for the sermon to be an oral event will not model the sermon after a finely honed literary essay or a chapter in a book of systematic theology, but will think of the sermon as a living conversation with the congregation. This may be difficult initially for pastors who have been trained in four years of undergraduate school and three or more years of seminary, the principal instrument of education being the long paper with style and format prescribed by a rigid style sheet. But Kate L. Turbian is not the best coach in "living" speech. No, the best preparation for oral style is simply to pay attention to the way in which people talk, to those modes of expression and vocal qualities that seem to cut nearest to the heart.

The most important practical consideration when one is getting together the actual words of the sermon is to be governed by a simple principle: prepare the sermon for the ear. If one is preparing a manuscript or notes, one can apply a simple test to every phrase, sentence, and paragraph: Is this expressed the way I would say it if I were talking to a group of friends? (And, indeed, the preacher will soon be talking to such a group!) Preaching can have all of the qualities of oral speech mentioned above, from explosive expletives to sentence fragments.[106]

Oral quality is not determined by the presence or absence of a manuscript. One preacher can speak without notes and have all the life of a computer-generated message. Another preacher can speak from a full manuscript in the pulpit and talk like the play-by-play announcer of the Nebraska Cornhuskers. Attitude, preparation, discipline, and delivery make the difference.[107]

Diagnostic Question

15. What are the indications in the sermon itself that this sermon is truly an oral event? What are the indications that it may not be an oral event?

16. A Good Title Is Inviting

A good title has positive value for the hearer, the potential hearer, and the preacher. It can spark the potential hearer to think, "Something interesting is going on at worship this Sunday. Maybe it will even be important for my life!" Especially if the title appears in the media prior to Sunday, it signals that the preacher is giving serious and extended thought to the sermon. A good title also gives the preacher a focus on the development of the sermon and can even stir the preacher's imagination. By raising the sense of expectation with which the congregation comes to worship, both preaching and worship becomes more satisfying for both preacher and worshipers.

The title should be used in the media beyond the boundaries of the local congregation.[108] In the newspaper, on radio, and on television, the title might be accompanied by a sentence or two (or more) saying something provocative about the major thrust of the sermon. Of course, such commentary should neither summarize the content of the sermon nor promise more than the sermon will actually deliver.

Many newspaper readers will see the church's material if it appears in the most frequently read sections of the paper. The religious "ghetto" (snooze) usually is not one of those sections. And more readers will notice the church's material if it is attractively, creatively, and freshly designed each week than if it is a dull, repetitive notice that the doors of the church will be open each Sunday at 9:00 a.m. (yawn). If a congregation's ad is forced onto the church page, a provocative title will stand out as a flower among the weeds.

More people will be exposed to the church's use of radio and television "spots" appearing in good time slots than if they are tucked away among the midnight public service announcements. If the material is thoughtfully planned and put together, it will attract more attention than if it sounds like a stock market report. Yet, even among the public service announcements, a good title and accompanying commentary may reach out of the screen and say, "Psst! Listen to this."

56

The title and appropriate scripture readings belong in the church paper with a brief but pointed paragraph drawing the attention of the congregation to the promise of the sermon. The worship bulletin is also a place for the title. A few words in a title can strike a deep and responsive chord in a listener.

A good title has five characteristics:

1. It is brief, usually no more than seven words.
2. It is directly related to the theme of the sermon. (But it does not give the sermon away.)
3. It is provocative and suggests that the sermon is related to the life of the listener.
4. It contains an image that begins to unlock the imagination of the listener.
5. It is stated positively.

Among examples of good titles (and their authors) are the following:

> Praying Through Clenched Teeth (Fred Craddock)
> God Within the Shadows (Eugene Brice)
> And How Does It All End? (Edmund Steimle)
> News from Another Network (David H. C. Read)
> The God Who Came in Out of the Cold (William Mehl)
> Journey in Search of a Soul (Frederick Buechner)

Poor titles typically have characteristics like the following. They give the whole sermon away, usually in a dreary, matter-of-fact way. They sound more like they belong in a lecture hall than in the sanctuary, e.g., "The Ground of Our Being in Its Veiling and Unveiling." Too general, they are like a pasture without a fence, e.g., "Love." They do not seem to be significant for the lives of the listeners, or they are couched in obscure religious language. Some are just plain dull, and others promise too much: "The Meaning of Faith," "The Three Steps to Peace of Mind." If there are only three steps, and if they can be explained adequately in a twenty-minute sermon, I would certainly like to know what they are.

Diagnostic Question

16. Put yourself in the position of a listener. How would you respond to the title of the sermon?

17. The Preacher Respects the Time of the Listener

Three phenomena coalesce to argue for keeping the sermon lean, muscular, and brief: the time allowed by the listener, the attention span of the listener, and the nature of the service of worship.

The cliché is right: "Time is one of our most important commodities." With the ever-increasing number of opportunities for (and demands upon) the use of time, and the ever-increasing pace of life, it is important for the leaders of worship and the preacher to respect the time of the listener. Herb Miller pungently says, "Many people who attend mainline churches, especially males, find their anger point rising toward ignition as the clock moves past twelve noon." A service of worship that goes beyond one hour is "grand larceny." "Preachers who break in and steal, regardless of their profound insights, will meet passive/aggressive resistance."[109] At their worst, those who resist will stay away from worship.

A normal attention span of the average listener has been reduced by television. Commercial advertisements sell not just a product but a world view in thirty seconds. The longest television segments are seldom more than eight minutes and often as short as five minutes. Many North Americans are thereby conditioned to think in blocks of brief, fast-changing segments of time. Even the newsweeklies, *Time* and *Newsweek*, digest issues of cosmic importance into a couple of paragraphs.

As already indicated, the sermon and service of worship cannot be modeled on the world of television (or *Newsweek*). But, the longer the service, the less likely are the participants to stay "tuned in."

The service of worship is wonderfully full, including weekly sermon, prayers, readings from the Bible, and, among denominations like the Christian Church (Disciples of Christ), the Lord's Supper. When the whole service is carefully planned and moves in a purposeful, elegant, and unhurried way, it can rise to a crest of authentic spiritual power. But in order for this to happen, the elements of the service need to be kept in balance.

Given these conditions, how long should the sermon be? Twenty minutes is probably the maximum length. Fifteen minutes is closer to the optimum, especially when the Lord's Supper is served.[110] On festival days (like Easter) when the service is especially full, the sermon may be as brief as ten minutes.[111]

Brevity means hard work for the preacher at the point of preparation. The sermon needs to move in an interesting and swift way to the major issue. The proportion of the sermon can be developed like the muscles of the body so that each part becomes the right size and shape for its purpose in the sermon. A lean, well-trained, and powerful runner can run hard for fifteen minutes and not even work up a sweat. Indeed, limitation is a desirable pattern throughout sermon preparation. First is limitation to a carefully defined purpose. Then follows the desire to be *simple* and creative, then the limitation on purposeless repetition in the sermon, and finally the limitation of time.

A danger accompanies the delivery of a sermon. Because of the pressure of time, the preacher may feel the need to rush the sermon. At the end, the congregation is tense and tired.

Brevity can also help the preacher. Given the limited amount of time, the preacher will want to get at the heart of the matter. "Since I have only fifteen minutes to talk with the congregation about this subject, what are the most important things needing to be said?" Both preacher and congregation are thereby saved from interesting, but distracting sideshows.

Diagnostic Exercise

17. How long does it take to preach this sermon in a live congregational setting?

18. The Sermon Is Delivered in a Warm and Genuine Way

As we saw earlier (Section 15), the delivery of the sermon is not just the "package" of the thought of the sermon. Only in the moment of delivery does the prepared text (whether written or oral) become a sermon. When the content of the sermonic text and the delivery of the text are consonant, the sermon is able to carry the full weight of its point to the congregation.

When the content and delivery are in conflict, the sermon sends the congregation confusing signals. For example, a message on love delivered with a clenched fist is a contradiction. A sermon on joy delivered in a flat, dull fashion communicates the wrong impression of Christian joy.

Three qualities are especially important in the delivery of the sermon: sincerity, passion, and naturalness.[112] Sincerity is perceived as the sense that the message is coming from the heart of the preacher and not just from the page. The passionate sermon is delivered with fire and conviction appropriate to the content. The listener can tell that the sermon is important to the preacher. Naturalness is the quality of being oneself in the pulpit. The natural preacher uses gestures and tone of voice continuous with the way in which one would speak in the hallway. To be sure, the act of preaching in the sanctuary will often call forth largeness of voice and gesture, but these need not be fake or even forced if they rise from the heart and are well practiced.

Listeners cite the following clues in delivery that they interpret as characteristics of the sincere sermon:[113]

1. Good eye contact, especially at key moments in the sermon;
2. Relative freedom from notes;
3. A clear, firm voice giving a definite, secure beginning and ending to the sermon;
4. A natural tone of voice, even when one is projecting;
5. Vocal variety, that is, the full and varied use of the voice from the lower ranges to the higher;

6. Ability to be heard, especially nondistracting use of the public address system;
7. Open body posture, especially open hands, with gestures inviting the listener into the presence of the pulpit.
8. Facial expressions that are alive and coordinated with what is being said;
9. Energy in the preacher;
10. A sense of surprise and wonder at the grace of God.

One of the most effective devices in preaching is the use of the pause. With striking power, the silence of the pause can underline a point, write an exclamation point in the mind of the listener, and give the congregation time to let a thought or an image come to rest in its consciousness. Of course, the pause must be controlled and intentional.

Listeners report the inverse of the positive characteristics as traits of delivery affecting them negatively. Too much reliance on the notes, especially reading from the notes, is the death of the sermon. "Preacher's voice," the habit of artificially inflecting words and phrases, and especially the habit of raising the voice at the end of the sentence, communicates artificiality of content, as well as of style. A motionless body and a blank face say, "I, the preacher, am not interested in this sermon." Facial expression and tone of voice contradicting the words being spoken may cause the listener to wonder if there are contradictions in the life of the preacher and even in God. The clenched fist, habitual shouting, and the incessant use of the pointed finger not only turn listeners off, but suggest that God is angry, shouting, and finger-pointing. I hasten to add that in a given context, for effect, the preacher may clench a fist, stand motionless, or point a finger, but when used routinely, such actions work against the sermon.

The preacher who takes the sermon seriously will practice the delivery. Preaching the sermon on Friday to the empty pews in the sanctuary is an excellent discipline. This helps get the sermon in mind and gives the preacher a feel for how the sermon will preach in the place of worship. Preaching through the sermon also helps one get a sense of the timing of the delivery. Rough spots can be discovered while there is still time to put them under the rolling pin. Speaking aloud will allow the preacher to adjust the length of the sermon to the time allotted for Sunday morning.

Indeed, one measure of the seriousness with which the preacher takes the sermon is the degree of preparation for delivery.[114]

Diagnostic Exercise

18. Recall the way the sermon was delivered (or think forward to the way in which the sermon will be delivered). Is the style of delivery appropriate to the content, and does the delivery enhance its reception by the hearer?

19. The Invitation to Discipleship Is Strong and Positive

The custom of many communions has long been to conclude the sermon with an invitation to discipleship. Even when "the invitation" and the sermon have been disconnected, the invitation has usually been continued at another point in the service.[115]

The theological underpinning of this practice is the notion that the word of God begets a response. In the sacred space and time of worship, we represent with symbolic gesture the response of our whole lives to the gospel. While this notion has been consistent in the history of the church, the nature of the response has differed from era to era and from church to church. For example, the response is sometimes a hymn, sometimes an affirmation of faith, sometimes the making of a new resolution to live in accord with the gospel, sometimes an offering and the Lord's Supper.

Such occasions offer pastoral guidance in at least three important respects. First, they are intentional moments in which the congregation is asked to consider its personal responses to the gospel of God. They help the congregation make a choice (see No. 10 above). Second, the congregation can act out its resolve, making announcement in the public arena of the worshiping community. By so doing, it solidifies the intention to live within the boundaries of the decision. And, third, by making a public witness, members gain the support of the whole community.

The invitation offers the congregation several significant opportunities: (1) Those who have never made a confession of faith and have never been baptized may make such a confession and indicate their desire to be baptized; (2) those who are already Christian and are seeking a new congregational home may transfer the record of their membership into the congregation; (3) others may wish to make a public reaffirmation of their faith; (4) still others may wish to come to the front of the church and to offer grateful testimony to God and to the church for blessings they have received; (5) many will use the invitation as a time to commit themselves silently to the ideas advanced in the sermon or to commit themselves anew to live for God; (6) during the invitation, some may pray for those who have not accepted the grace of God; and (7) in some congregations, those seeking special prayers (such as prayer for healing) may come forward.

When the invitation is given in the mainline churches, usually it is dignified and without emotional excess. Seldom do mainliners put the mind in neutral and push the pedal on the emotions to the floorboard. Indeed, if anything, many mainline pastors show such restraint that the invitation becomes *pro forma*. I have been in services in which no one, not even the pastor, seemed to expect anyone to come forward, and I have even seen ministers who appeared embarrassed by the act of giving the invitation.

Those who issue the call of God at the time of the invitation can enhance the call and the whole service by giving careful attention to the way in which it is done. In addition to giving the invitation in such a way as to maintain the integrity, artistry, and movement of the service, it can be given in a joyful and confident manner as befits *an invitation from God!*[116]

A matter for special consideration is the transition from the sermon to the invitation. Most sermons will naturally come to the point of asking the listener, either directly or indirectly, to make a choice concerning the major thrust of the sermon. Is it for me? The preacher will help the congregation by letting it see the clear issues involved and by putting the choice before them.

But some sermons are of content and stylistic wholeness that do not naturally issue in such choices. In these cases, the pastor may want to let the sermon rise to its own crest, pause for a few moments of silence while the sermon soaks in, perhaps offer a brief prayer, and then state the invitation. The preacher may be able honorably to pick up an image from the sermon as part of the invitation. And the transition from message to invitation may be facilitated if the minister moves from the pulpit to the center of the chancel. In fact, this move may give the invitation a warmer, more personal character.

Diagnostic Exercise

19. Review the invitation given (or planned to be given) with the sermon. How is it appropriate to the message and to the gospel?

20. Feedback Improves Communication

The literature of communication theory describes communication as a process involving five basic steps:

1. The speaker (preacher) prepares a message intended to have a certain effect on the receivers (congregation).
2. The speaker sends the message to the receivers.
3. The people receive the message and interpret its meaning for themselves.
4. The receivers send feedback to the speaker. The feedback says things like, "We understand this message and we like it!" "We understand this message and we do not like it." "We do not understand this message."
5. The speaker receives the feedback and adjusts the presentation of the message to account for the feedback.[117]

The process of communication is an incomplete circle until the speaker has been able to assess the relative success of the communicated message.

The feedback received by most preachers is of two kinds. One is during the actual preaching itself. The expressions on the faces of the congregation and their attentiveness are signs of whether or not the message is getting through. If, for example, the congregation is plainly uninterested or confused, the preacher can take corrective steps in the course of the sermon. However, confident interpretation of congregational signals is not always possible during the sermon. Does a wrinkled face mean confusion about what the preacher is saying or annoyance at some mannerism of the speaker? Does it mean hostility toward the content of the sermon or even toward the person of the preacher? Or is the person with the wrinkled face about to sneeze?

The other kind of feedback typically received by the preacher is at the door of the sanctuary. Significant encounters can transpire in moments at the door. Yet, while the usual greetings are sincere and gratifying, they do little to help the preacher know the blocks or aids to the communication of the message.

Several simple things can be done to yield careful, thoughtful reflection on the sermon.[118] Although these things take place after the actual event of preaching, regular attention to them can help the pastor interpret feedback in the moment of preaching and preparation for the next sermon.

A sermon feedback group is especially helpful. The preacher assembles a group of perceptive people in the congregation and asks them to meet weekly for a period of time in order to reflect on the way the sermon was communicated. Through the use of written response forms and/or group discussion, the group can articulate what got through, what did not, and why. They can identify particular strengths and weaknesses of the pastor's style. They can point to barriers in communication, and an alert group can suggest ways the preacher might want to do things differently in the future. Such a group can help make the pastor aware of local idiosyncrasies and customs affecting how the sermon is received. Some pastors have found it especially helpful to videotape the sermon and to play the tape during the feedback session.

In the initial stages, members are sometimes reluctant to speak critically of the sermon. When the pastor is not defensive, but responds to criticism in an open and probing way, the people gradually begin to open up. As the trust of the group grows, the feedback can become frank and honest, and ultimately it can strengthen the preaching ministry. From time to time, the leader may need to remind participants that their first obligation is not to deal with the content of the sermon as content, but to help the preacher understand his or her style of communication.

If it proves difficult to get a group together, individuals in the congregation can be commissioned as sermon critics. Some members, such as speech teachers and attorneys, have well-developed critical capacities to bring to their assignments.

Videotaping can be done very unobtrusively and to eye-opening benefit. Taping apparatus can be set up in a balcony or on a side aisle, adjusted for focus and volume, turned on, and left to run. After getting over the schock of seeing and hearing themselves on the screen, pastors will have no trouble seeing whether their style is communicative or noncommunicative. (The camera does not lie.) If the church does not own taping equipment, the equipment can be borrowed from a parishioner, school, or business. Some pastors now send videotapes to pulpit committees when the latter request a tape of a sermon.

The regular use of an audiotape is easy, inexpensive, and convenient for replay. A pastor can even listen to the tape while driving to and from pastoral calls. The audiotape reveals much about the use of the voice, pace, timing, intensity, and the flow of the ideas of the sermon.

The use of a feedback mechanism does invite one caution. The preacher who takes feedback seriously can easily and unconsciously slip into the pattern of changing things in order to please the feedback group. The goal of using a feedback group is not to please the committee but to learn how to communicate a message clearly. Only then will listeners be able to decide properly whether to accept or to reject the messages.

Diagnostic Exercise

20. Arrange for a sermon feedback group to meet for six weeks.

Catalogue of Diagnostic Questions and Exercises

1. What does this sermon say about God?
    a. Is it appropriate to the gospel?
    b. Is it intelligible?
2. In this sermon, what is the good news from God for the congregation?
3. What is the fundamental life issue with which this sermon is concerned?
4. Does the Bible appear in a prominent and appropriate place in this sermon?
5. What, in this sermon, is an authoritative word for our time? Why could it be regarded as having authority?
6. How does this sermon communicate the offer of salvation?
7. Put the sermon into a simple, indicative sentence. What do you hope this sermon will accomplish in the lives of the listeners?
8. What is the evidence that this sermon is basically indicative?
9. In this sermon, what are the signals that it is addressed from person to person?
10. How does this sermon help the listener come to a decision about the gospel?
11. What are the concrete elements in this sermon?
12. How does humor in this sermon serve the major point?
13. With a red pencil, mark the elements of graphic speech in the sermon.
    a. In this sermon, what does the listener:
        (1) See?
        (2) Hear?
        (3) Touch?
        (4) Taste?
        (5) Smell?
    b. How do the elements of graphic speech help the sermon achieve its purpose?
    c. Does any of the graphic language call attention to itself?
    d. Where in the sermon could more graphic speech be used?
14. Create and complete an inclusivity grid like the one on p. 52.

15. What are the indications in the sermon itself that this sermon is truly an oral event? What are the indications that it may not be an oral event?
16. Put yourself in the position of a listener. How would you respond to the title of the sermon?
17. How long does it take to preach this sermon in a live congregational setting?
18. Recall the way the sermon was delivered (or think forward to the way in which the sermon will be delivered). Was the style of delivery appropriate to the content?
19. Review the invitation given (or planned to be given) with the sermon. How is it appropriate to the message and to the gospel?
20. Arrange for a sermon feedback group to meet for six weeks.

Ten Books on Preaching
Every Preacher Ought to Read

These ten books are listed because they represent the best of a variety of contemporary approaches to preaching. All contain detailed bibliography for further study.

Achtemeier, Elizabeth, *Creative Preaching*. Abingdon, 1980. In this basic work, "creative" refers not to the new and different but to the power of the word to create that which it speaks.

Buechner, Frederick, *Telling the Truth: The Gospel as Tragedy, Comedy and Fairy Tale*. Harper and Row, 1977. With inimitable prose, Buechner uses the literary techniques of tragedy, comedy, and fairy tale as ways of helping us understand how the gospel comes to us. The preacher's business is to tell the truth concerning the tragedy, the comedy, and the fairy tale.

Buttrick, David G., *Homiletic: Moves and Structures*. Fortress, 1987. Although this book arrived on my desk too late to be used as a resource for the present work, its appearance is a once-in-a-lifetime event. Buttrick has read everything and says everything, but in a charming and winsome way. His fresh proposal is to see the sermon as a series of carefully considered "moves." The bibliographies are exhaustive and alone worth the price of the book.

Craddock, Fred B., *As One Without Authority*. Abingdon, 1979, o.p. 1971. One of the most important works presents "inductive preaching." Craddock's style of writing is a model for preachers.

——————— , *Overhearing the Gospel*. Abingdon, 1978. Craddock argues that the most effective posture for preacher and listener is to "overhear" the gospel.

——————— , *Preaching*. Abingdon, 1985. With Buttrick's *Homiletic*, this is one of the two best introductions to preaching.

Lowry, Eugene L., *The Homiletical Plot*. John Knox, 1980. The "Lowry loop" is presented as the model for the structure of the sermon. The "loop" moves from upsetting the equilibrium of the listener to experiencing the gospel.

Steimle, Edmund; Rice, Charles; and Niedenthal, Morris. *Preaching the Story*. Fortress, 1980. This is the most complete exposition of the notion of "sermon as story."

Van Seters, Arthur, editor, *Preaching as a Social Act*. Abingdon, 1988. Several teachers of preaching consider the social dimensions of preaching and illustrate their discoveries with sermons.

Wardlaw, Don M., editor, *Preaching Biblically*. Westminster, 1983. A series of essays and sermons illustrates how the shape of scripture can shape the sermon.

Notes

1. Herb Miller, *Fishing on the Asphalt* (CBP Press, 1983), pp. 101-111; Kennon L. Callahan, *Twelve Keys to an Effective Church* (Harper and Row, 1983), pp. 28-29; C. Peter Wagner, *Leading Your Church to Growth* (GL Publications, 1984), pp. 215-218; Joe M. Harding, *Have I Told You Lately . . .?* (Church Growth Press, 1982); and Earl V. Comfort, "Is the Pulpit a Factor in Church Growth?" in *Bibliotheca Sacra* 140 (1983), pp. 64-70.

2. Discussion of this topic can be found in: Frank J. Matera, "Gospel," in *Harper's Bible Dictionary*, ed. Paul J. Achtemeier (Harper and Row, 1985), pp. 354-55; Fred B. Craddock, "Preaching," in *Harper's Bible Dictionary*, p. 818; O. A. Piper, "Gospel (Message)," in *The Interpreter's Dictionary of the Bible*, ed. George A. Buttrick (Abingdon, 1964), vol. 2, pp. 442-448; and Gerhard Friedrich, "euangelizomai," in *Theological Dictionary of the New Testament*, ed. Gerhard Kittel, tr. Geoffrey Bromiley (Eerdmans, 1964), vol. II, pp. 707-737. Cf. Gerhard Friedrich, "kerux," in *Theological Dictionary of the New Testament*, vol. III, pp. 683-717.

3. In the Hebrew Bible, the root most often associated with "good news" is *bsr*. This root also can be simply "news" or "tidings." In the Septuagint, the *bsr* group is usually rendered by the *euangel* family. See 1 Samuel 4:17, 31:9, 2 Samuel 1:20, 1 Chronicles 10:9, 1 Kings 1:43.

4. 11b, "great . . . tidings" might also be translated, "The women who bore the good news are a great company," as in *Today's English Version*.

5. A particularly important essay is: Carl R. Holladay, "Church Growth in the New Testament: Some Historical Considerations and Theological Perspectives," in *Restoration Quarterly* 26 (1983), pp. 85-102.

6. It goes almost without saying that in the biblical tradition, evangelism can be thought of as action as well as announcement. In fact, an action can be an announcement of the good news, as in the case of the Markan exorcisms. Actions, however, must be interpreted so that their meaning can be made clear.

7. For the sake of brevity, I have greatly simplified the notion(s) of covenant in Israel. For fuller discussions, see E. W. Nicholson, *God and His People: Covenant and Theology in the Old Testament* (Oxford, 1986); and Jon Levenson, *Sinai and Zion* (Winston-Seabury, 1985). Briefer treatment may be found in: Jeremiah Untermann, "Covenant," in *Harper's Bible Dictionary*, pp. 190-192; G. E. Mendenhall, "Covenant," in *The Interpreter's Dictionary of the Bible*, vol. 1, pp. 714-723; Gottfried Quell and Johannes Behm, "diatithemi," in *Theological Dictionary of the New Testament*, vol. II, pp. 104-133; M. Weinfeld, "Covenant, Davidic," in *The Interpreter's Dictionary of the Bible (Supplement)*, ed. Keith Crim, et. al. (Abingdon, 1976), pp. 188-192; and Paul A. Rieman, "Covenant, Mosaic," in *The Interpreter's Dictionary of the Bible (Supplement)* pp. 192-197.

8. On the prophetic office, the following summaries are useful introductions: Robert R. Wilson, "Prophet," in *Harper's Bible Dictionary*, pp. 826-830; B. D. Napier, "Prophet," in *The Interpreter's Dictionary of the Bible*, vol. 3, pp. 896-919; Helmut Kraemer, et. al., "prophetes," in *Theological Dictionary of the*

New Testament, vol. VI, pp. 781-861; and M.J. Buss, "Prophecy in Ancient Israel," in *The Interpreter's Dictionary of the Bible (Supplement)*, pp. 694-697.

9. Sander's basic idea is repeated and developed in several of his writings, e.g., "Hermeneutics," in *The Interpreter's Dictionary of the Bible (Supplement)*, pp. 402-407; *idem., God Has a Story Too* (Fortress, 1979), pp. 17-26; *idem., Canon and Community* (Fortress, 1984). Many of Sanders' leading essays are now brought together in his *From Sacred Story to Sacred Text* (Fortress, 1987).

10. I have given more detailed consideration to this topic in "The Relationship Between the Pastoral and the Prophetic in Preaching," in *Encounter* (forthcoming).

11. Augustine, *On Christian Doctrine*, tr. J. F. Shaw, *Nicene and Post Nicene Fathers*, ed. Philip Schaff (Christian Literature Company, 1887), Book I.22, 31-32, esp. 35, 38. Note that for Augustine, "doctrine" refers to preaching!

12. Martin Luther, "The Babylonian Captivity of the Church," tr. A. T. W. Steinhaeuser, F. C. Ahrens, and A. R. Wentz, *Luther's Works*, ed., A. R. Wentz (Muhlenburg, 1959), vol. 36, p. 116.

13. John Calvin, *Institutes of the Christian Religion*, ed. John McNeill, tr. Ford Battles (Westminster, 1960), IV.1.

14. *Millennial Harbinger*, VI (1835), p. 351. Cf. Granville T. Walker, *Preaching in the Thought of Alexander Campbell* (Bethany Press, 1954), pp. 40, 156-161.

15. *Millennial Harbinger*, XXV (1854), p. 304. Cf. Walker, *Ibid.*, pp. 162-166.

16. Campbell's model holds promise for the church today. Few of the unconverted come to the church building or to mass meetings in order to be exposed to the gospel. It makes sense, therefore, that the heart of the evangelistic witness of the church should be made by Christians in everyday traffic. The Sunday sermon would then be seen clearly as an occasion in which the congregation is instructed in the Christian faith and thereby prepared for witness. In the mainline church as it is now, the evangelistic witness is being made with remarkably little force and congregations are not being fed enough solid food.

Much of the church growth movement is very helpful but is more properly characterized as membership recruitment than as evangelistic witness. Few church-growth-movement materials prepare a congregation to speak with the unconverted. Popular materials preparing people to talk with other people about the Christian faith tend to be inadequate or inappropriate.

Members of the church live decent, moral lives, perhaps believing that most people would rather see a sermon than hear one any day. Or they simply may be uninformed about the importance of making a Christian witness, or, they may be too frightened to speak. Whatever the reason, members of the mainline churches give little explicit testimony to those who are strangers to God, in either private or public encounter.

Much of the preaching that I hear as I travel around spends a disproportionate amount of its homiletical energy addressing the "issues of the day" in a moralistic fashion (telling people what to do and how to vote) but with remarkably little attention to basic Christian conviction concerning the human condition and the initiative of God. (See No. 8) The sermon, then, is neither evangelistic toward those who do not believe, nor is it spiritually nourishing for the already

71

converted.

Thus, the church's evangelistic witness is lost and its religious hunger is not fed with solid food. Campbell's clear delineation offers a possible corrective.

17. D. Newell Williams, *The Theology of the Great Revival in the West As Seen Through the Life and Thought of Barton Warren Stone* (Unpublished Ph.D. Dissertation, Vanderbilt University, 1979), pp. 161-162.

18. Elder John Rogers, *The Biography of Eld. Barton Warren Stone, Written by Himself: with Additions and Reflections* (Published for the Author by J. A. and U. P. James, 1847), reprinted in Hoke S. Dickinson, ed., *The Cane Ridge Reader* (N.P., 1872), pp. 10-11.

19. Pieter de Jong, *Evangelism and Contemporary Theology* (Tidings, 1962), p. 111. The theologians on the basis of whose work de Jong comes to this conclusion are Reinhold Niebuhr, Paul Tillich, Dietrich Bonhoeffer, Emil Brunner, Karl Barth, and Rudolf Bultmann.

20. Clark M. Williamson, "Preaching the Gospel: Some Theological Reflections" (1985) (Unpublished manuscript).

21. Although the need for brevity precludes a discussion and evaluation of the major expressions of evangelism in our time, mention should be made of two bodies of literature that enter substantially into any discussion of evangelism today. The Commission on World Mission and Evangelism of the World Council of Churches calls attention to the "monstrosity" of sin alienating "persons from God, neighbours and nature," and "found both in individual and corporate forms, both in slavery of the human will and in social, political and economic structures of domination and dependence." In this context, "the church is sent into the world to call people and nations to repentance, to announce forgiveness of sin and a new beginning in relations with God and neighbors through Jesus Christ." [*Mission and Evangelism: An Ecumenical Affirmation*, ed. Jean Stromberg (World Council of Churches, 1983), p. 1.] In this comprehensive understanding, the gospel is to be proclaimed to every person and social system, and may be proclaimed in word as well as in service.

The Church Growth Movement distinguishes between two mandates given by God to the church. One is a cultural mandate that calls for the promotion of shalom among persons, nations, and nature. "Distribution of wealth, the balance of nature, marriage and the family, human government, keeping the peace, cultural integrity, liberation of the oppressed—these and other responsibilities rightly fall within the cultural mandate." [C. Peter Wagner, *Church Growth and the Whole Gospel* (Harper and Row, 1981), p. 13.] The other mandate is the evangelistic mandate whose purpose is to present Jesus persuasively so that women and men will accept him as Savior and, through him, serve God in the church. *Ibid.*, p. 57. Note that "*kingdom growth* is the ultimate task of the church while *church growth* is the penultimate task" (p. 59). On this discussion cf. Gerald H. Anderson and Thomas F. Stransky, *Mission Trends No. 1.* (Paulist; William B. Eerdmans, 1974), esp. A. F. Glasser and Tracey K. Jones, Jr., "What is 'Mission' Today? Two Views," pp. 5-12; Anderson and Stransky, *Mission Trends No. 2: Evangelization* (1975).

22. Hans van der Geest, *Presence in the Pulpit*, tr. Douglas W. Stott (John Knox, 1981), p. 57.

23. Williamson (Unpublished manuscript). Cf. David Tracy, *Blessed Rage*

72

for Order (Seabury, 1975), pp. 72ff.

24. *Ibid.*

25. In the case of this example, note that some believers attempt to make faith foolproof by rationalization of "unanswered prayer." Perhaps, they say, the fault is not with God or with the preacher but with the one who prayed: that person (or community) did not have enough faith. Perhaps God did answer the prayer, but answered it "No." Perhaps the negative result is because "God knows best," so that all we can do is bear misfortune and tragedy with stoicism. Perhaps God was intending to teach us "a lesson." If so, what is taught other than the unreliability of God? Such reasoning hardly enhances the credibility of belief in God.

26. Gordon Kaufman, *God the Problem* (Harvard, 1972).

27. Edmund A. Steimle, *God the Stranger* (Fortress, 1979), p. 73.

28. For a fascinating treatment of this subject, see: George Lakhoff and Mark Johnson, *Metaphors We Live By* (University of Chicago, 1980).

29. This image is suggested by my colleague, D. Newell Williams.

30. From Peter Berger and Thomas Luckmann, *The Social Construction of Reality* (Doubleday, 1966), among others, one can infer that a basic purpose of preaching is to posit a "symbolic universe" investing life with meaning. This has been a purpose of religion since the dawn of consciousness. From another perspective, Susanne K. Langer, *Philosophy In a New Key* (Harvard, 1942), pp. 144-203.

31. An important guide to the ethos of modern life is: Robert N. Bellah, Richard Madsen, William M. Sullivan, Ann Swindler, and Stephen Tipton, *Habits of the Heart* (University of California, 1985).

32. Leander Keck, *The Bible in the Pulpit* (Abingdon, 1978, pp. 53ff.).

33. I am convinced that expository preaching (understood as the exposition of the significance of a biblical text or theme in the light of the gospel for the modern world) is the basic mode of parish preaching.

34. For a summary of the issues at stake, see: Paul J. Achtemeier, *The Inspiration of Scripture* (Westminster, 1980); James Barr, *The Scope and Authority of the Bible* (Westminster, 1980); David L. Bartlett, *The Shape of Scriptural Authority* (Fortress, 1983); William Countryman, *Biblical Authority or Biblical Tyranny* (Fortress, 1981); Kenneth Hagen, ct. al., *The Bible in the Churches* (Paulist, 1985); and Letty M. Russel, ed., *Feminist Interpretation of the Bible* (Westminster, 1985).

35. See: Alene Stuart Phy, *The Bible in Popular Culture* (Fortress, 1984).

36. An organization that has developed introductory level material for Bible study is the Institute for Biblical Literacy, 337 S. Milledge Ave., Suite 218, Athens, GA 30605.

37. This approach is developed further in: William J. Nottingham, *The Practice and Preaching of Liberation* (CBP Press, 1986), pp. 43-46.

38. Ronald J. Allen, "Preaching Against the Text," in *Encounter* 48 (1987), pp. 105-116.

39. The lectionary most widely used in the last years of the twentieth century is the *Common Lectionary* (Church Hymnal Corporation, 1983).

40. More detailed evaluations of lectionaries can be found in: Lloyd R. Bailey, "The Lectionary in Critical Perspective," in *Interpretation* 31 (1977), pp.

139-153; William Skudlarek, *The Word in Worship* (Abingdon, 1981), esp. pp. 11-64; James A. Sanders, "Canon and Calendar: An Alternative Lectionary Proposal," in *Social Themes of the Christian Year*, ed. by Dieter T. Hessel (Geneva Press, 1983), pp. 257-263; and *Handbook for the Common Lectionary*, ed. by Peter C. Bower (Geneva Press, 1987), pp. 15-30.

41. In addition to the critique mentioned above, cf. Justo L. Gonzalez and Catherine L. Gonzalez, *Liberation Preaching* (Abingdon, 1980), pp. 38-47.

42. Paul Lehmann's statement about certain movements in theological education, given to seniors graduating from a theological seminary, may also suggest why the church's recent voice has not been spoken (or heard) with more force. "In our present preoccupation with experience over tradition, with immediacy over understanding, with immanence over transcendence, with self-consciousness over obedience . . . we are risking sending you upon your several ministries with trumpets ill-equipped." "No Uncertain Sound," in *Union Seminary Quarterly Review* 29 (1974), p. 277.

43. For a penetrating analysis of the "collapse of the house of authority," see: Edward Farley, *Ecclesial Reflection* (Fortress, 1982).

44. William Baird, *What is Our Authority?*. (Christian Board of Publication, n.d.), p. 8.

45. For a proposal on apologetics, see: William J. Carl, *Preaching Christian Doctrine* (Fortress, 1984), pp. 95-138.

46. A simple way in which to use this method is to ask questions from the perspectives of these resources?

> What is the witness of Scripture?
> What is the witness of Christian tradition?
> What is the witness of experience?
> What is the witness of reason?
> Do these verify one another? Do they call one
>   another into question? Do they call for the
>   modification of the testimony of a witness?
> Are these witnesses appropriate to the gospel to which they
>   bear witness?

In preaching, one will often start with the claims of a text and ask how these claims have been understood in Christian tradition and how they are understood in experience and in the light of reason. When one is preaching on a topic generated from the modern context, Scripture and tradition may have little to say directly. When Scripture is directly silent, we may be able to reason analogically from a case in Scripture to the modern case, or to reason from hermeneutical principles established in Scripture. For instance, moderns may not be interested in the problem of food offered to idols (1 Corinthians 8), but our congregations may face questions that are analogous. Or, in a given situation, how would we apply the principle that Christ showed God's love by dying for *all*? Of course, we moderns need to be prepared for Scripture and tradition to *challenge* our view of reality.

47. Van der Geest, pp. 114-121.

48. *Ibid.*, pp. 40-45.

49. Aristotle, *The "Art" of Rhetoric*, tr. J. H. Freese, Loeb Classical Library (Harvard, 1932), II. 1.

50. Van der Geest, pp. 32ff. Cf. Fred B. Craddock, "Listening to the Listener," in *The Disciple*. October, 1984, p. 19.

51. A concise statement of noteworthy issues concerning the doctrine of salvation is: Walter Lowe, "Christ and Salvation," in *Christian Theology*, ed. Peter Hodgson and Robert King (Fortress, 1985), pp. 222-248.

52. The Bible and Christian tradition contain many different names (each with a different nuance) which point to a similar reality, e.g., salvation, the sovereign rule (RSV: kingdom) of God, new heaven and new earth, and perfection.

53. Van der Geest, pp. 71-74.

54. Keith Watkins, "Four Worship Needs," in *The Disciple*. November, 1984, p. 25.

55. Fred B. Craddock, *As One Without Authority* (Abingdon, 1971).

56. Edmund A. Steimle, Charles L. Rice, Morris J. Niedenthal, *Preaching the Story* (Fortress, 1980).

57. Keck, p. 102.

58. H. H. Farmer, *The Servant of the Word* (Fortress, 1964, o.p. 1942), p. 22.

59. Martin Buber, *I and Thou*. Second Edition. Tr. Ronald Gregor Smith (Charles Scribner's Sons, 1958). For discussion of the implications of the I-Thou relationship to preaching, cf. Farmer, pp. 21-64, esp. 21-36.

60. Still worth considering in this regard are: Reuel Howe, *Partners in Preaching* (Seabury, 1967); Dietrich Ritschl, *A Theology of Proclamation* (John Knox, 1960); and Rudolph Bohren, *Preaching and Community*, tr. David Green (John Knox, 1965). Cf. Van der Geest, *Ibid.*, pp. 88-91.

61. For a summary of the present state of discussion, see: Langdon Gilkey, "God," in *Christian Theology*, pp. 88-113.

62. Van der Geest, *Ibid.*, p. 61. Van der Geest does not use the term "I-Thou."

63. Farmer, *Ibid.*, pp. 43-44. Cf. Van der Geest, pp. 40-41, 46-47.

64. Of course, the word "we" need not be avoided altogether. It can be used effectively when it is used carefully. For example, "I suppose at one time or another we all feel that way."

65. Charles L. Rice, "The Preacher's Story," in *Preaching the Story*, pp. 19-36. Richard L. Eslinger takes the opposite point of view. Eslinger, depending upon research by David G. Buttrick, writes, "Most first-person stories do not serve their intended purposes of demonstrating solidarity with the congregation and providing an immediacy to the 'point.'" According to Eslinger, the first person story actually distances the preacher from the people. Richard Eslinger, "Story and Image in Sermon Illustration," in *Journal for Preachers*, vol. IX, no. 2 (1986), p. 19. Cf. David G. Buttrick, cited by Perry H. Biddle, "A Phenomenological Approach to Preaching," in *Sharing the Practice*, vol. 7, no. 4 (1984), p. 44.

66. Van der Geest, p. 149.

67. *Ibid.*, p. 129.

68. Elizabeth B. Howes and Sheila Moon, *The Choicemaker* (Theosophical Press, 1977), pp. 23-30.

69. Fred B. Craddock, *Overhearing the Gospel* (Abingdon, 1978).

70. Steimle, "The Fabric of the Sermon," in *Preaching the Story*, p. 172.

71. Throughout this section, I am indebted to Farmer, pp. 66-88.

72. Farmer, pp. 70-71.

73. Steimle, "The Fabric of the Sermon," in *Preaching the Story*, p. 174.

74. David G. Buttrick, "Homiletics and Rhetoric," (Lecture at Pittsburgh Theological Seminary, 1979), quoted in Carl, p. 29.

75. John Vannorsdall, "Humor as Content and Device in Preaching," in *Dialog* 22 (1983), pp. 187-188. The entire summer issue of *Dialog* (22) is devoted to humor. For a different approach, cf. John W. Drakeford, *Humor in Preaching* (Zondervan, 1986).

76. Morris J. Niedenthal, "The Comic Response to the Gospel: The Dethronement of the Powers." in *Papers of the Annual Meeting of the Academy of Homiletics (1985)*, p. 38.

77. Frederick Buechner, *Telling the Truth: The Gospel as Tragedy, Comedy and Fairy Tale* (Harper and Row, 1977), pp. 49-72.

78. James A. Sanders, *God Has a Story Too*, p. 24.

79. David G. Buttrick, cited by Perry H. Biddle, "A Phenomonological Approach to Preaching," p. 44.

80. Van der Geest, p. 127.

81. *Ibid.*, p. 128. As representative of a whole body of literature in which the power of graphic language is developed, see: Philip Wheelwright, *Metaphor and Reality* (University of Indiana, 1962).

82. On the relationship of language and world, see: Ronald J. Allen, "The Social Function of Language in Preaching" in *Preaching As A Social Act*, ed. by Arthur Van Seters (Abingdon, forthcoming). Cf. Berger and Luckmann; Walter Ong, *The Presence of the Word* (Yale, 1967); Ian G. Barbour, *Myths, Models and Paradigms* (Harper and Row, 1974); Northrup Frye, *The Great Code* (Harcourt, Brace, Jovanovich, 1982).

83. The term comes from Berger and Luckman.

84. The primary source of information about the world is sense data upon which the mind reflects.

85. Langer, pp. 79ff.

86. Langer, pp. 144ff.

87. Robert E. Ornstein, *The Psychology of Consciousness* (W. H. Freeman, 1972). For a more recent assessment see: Howard Stone, "Left Brain, Right Brain," in *Theology Today* 40 (1983), pp. 292-303, who gives bibliography. Studies in neuro-linguistic programming claim that each person thinks predominately in one of three ways: in visual images, in sounds, or in feelings. See: Richard Bandler and John Grinder, *Frogs into Princes* (Real People Press, 1979), pp. 14ff.

88. Fred B. Craddock, *As One Without Authority* (Abingdon, 1979, o.p. 1971), pp. 85-86.

89. A cheap notebook, habitually carried in pocket or purse, kept in the glove box and left on the night stand, provides a handy place to store images.

90. David Buttrick in "A Phenomenological Approach to Preaching," p. 44.

91. The literature on storytelling is vast. For a fine theological introduction, see: George Stroup, *The Promise of Narrative Theology* (John Knox, 1982). Cf. William J. Bausch, *Storytelling: Imagination and Faith* (Twenty-third Publications, 1984). Much creative work in storytelling is being done by the Network of

Biblical Storytellers (NOBS), 229 W. 78th Street, New York, NY 10024.

92. Van der Geest, p. 132.

93. *Ibid.*, p. 133.

94. *Ibid.*, p. 139.

95. A similar grid appears in: Allen, "The Social Function of Language in Preaching."

96. The literature on the subject of inclusive language is now immense. Reliable guides that work at the matter from different angles are: Keith Watkins, *Faithful and Fair* (Abingdon, 1981); Sallie McFague, *Metaphorical Theology* (Fortress, 1982); and Dianne Tennis, *Is God the Only Reliable Father?* (Westminster, 1985).

97. For further elaboration of this theme, see "The Social Function of Language in Preaching."

98. Among the guides for developing inclusive language patterns are: Keith Watkins, *Faithful and Fair*, esp. pp. 59-61; Letty M. Russell, ed., *The Liberating Word* (Westminster, 1976; William D. Watley, ed., *The Word and Words* (Consultation on Church Union, 1983); *Use of Inclusive Language in the Worship of the Church* (Wesley Theological Seminary, 1982); Marianne Sawicki, *Faith and Sexism: Guidelines for Religious Educators* (Seabury, 1979); and Nancy A. Hardesty, *Inclusive Language in the Church* (John Knox, 1987), who gives an extensive bibliography, pp. 103-109.

99. A special problem is posed by the language of the Bible. Of course, Hebrew, Greek, and Aramaic all contain words and expressions for humankind that have been rendered into English by the use of masculine terms (e.g., "he who . . ."). But most of these expressions can easily and legitimately be made inclusive (e.g., "the one who . . ."). The bigger problem is with other more technical expressions that are gender-specific in the original languages, e.g. Abba, Father. Can these legitimately be changed in the public reading of the Bible? I believe that to do so attacks the problem of inclusivity at the wrong level. The matter should be considered not at the level of translation but at the level of hermeneutics. The Bible is a historical document from a very different time, place, and world view, and it has its own historical integrity. The historical reality cannot be changed. We may wish that its language and imagery were something other than what they are, but we cannot change what happened in history. Instead, we can interpret the Bible theologically, honoring what it says but stating our own differing viewpoints. Public readers of the Bible can be trained to give interpretive introductions to the readings. On this issue, serious Christians disagree. A lectionary that is somewhat successful in reducing the number of "masculinisms" in the text is *Hearing the Word: An Inclusive Language Liturgical Lectionary* (Washington, D.C. 20010: St. Stephen and the Incarnation Episcopal Church, Box 43202, n.d.).

Bold in intent and to be appreciated as a pioneering work is *An Inclusive Language Lectionary* (John Knox, et.al., 1983, 1984, 1985), 3 vols. However this attempt is unsatisfying in style and in its treatment of historically-conditioned metaphors. See the review by Elizabeth Achtemeier in *Interpretation* 38 (1984), pp. 64-66.

100. One of the early and foundational works is by Ong. The most thoroughgoing attempt of a theologian to appropriate the insights which have

resulted from the study of orality is: Werner Kelber, *The Oral and the Written Gospel* (Fortress, 1983), describing the difficulties attendant upon the modern interpreter who is working with a written biblical text that was itself once oral but is now available to us only in written form. The works on homiletics by Fred Craddock are permeated by this concern; see especially *As One Without Authority* and *Preaching* (Abingdon, 1985).

101. Belden C. Lane, "The Oral Tradition and Its Implications for Preaching," in *Journal for Preachers* 7 (1984), no. 3, pp. 19-21.

102. *Ibid.*, p. 19.

103. *Ibid.*, p. 20.

104. *Ibid.*, p. 21.

105. The following are derived from Walter J. Ong, *Orality and Literacy* (Methuen Press, 1984), esp. pp. 31-77.

106. Readers will note some tension between the suggestion made in No. 4 above that worshipers should bring their Bibles to church in order to follow the text and the present stress on the orality of the sermon. We no longer live in an oral culture. While we can reclaim much of the force of orality in preaching, we can also draw upon the availability of the printed text. While the origins of much of the Bible are in oral tradition, the Bible as we have it *is* a printed text. Sensitive and creative preachers can make effective use of the Bible in the sermon as long as they remember that the sermon is primarily an oral event. In seminary classes on biblical exegesis, we work with the printed text, but the classes themselves often have the character of oral events!

107. If one preaches from a manuscript, it is advisable to develop a manuscript which in format does not look like an essay or a chapter in a book. Charles Rice suggests that his students follow the style

> made popular a few years ago by Peter Marshall
>   in which the preacher writes units of thought in a
>   descending way like this.
> This allows the eye of the preacher to follow
>   the material more easily and gives the manuscript an
>   "oral appearance."

See: Peter Marshall, *John Doe: Disciple* (McGraw-Hill, 1963); *Mr. Jones, Meet the Master* (Revell, 1949); and the sermons by Charles Rice, *Interpretation and Imagination* (Fortress, 1970). Clyde Fant has developed an elaborate program for the development of an "oral manuscript." *Preaching for Today* (Harper & Row, 1975).

108. On the use of the media by the church, see: Steve Dunkin, *Church Advertising* (Abingdon, 1982).

The announcement of the Sunday Service is not the only way to use the media. Many congregations have discovered that they can touch the nonbeliever (as well as persons simply looking for a church home) by the use of short creative advertisements in the newspaper or "spots" on the broadcast media containing a helpful, provocative thought about life. The purpose is to capture the attention of the audience and to attract them to worship. This makes use of contemporary media and preserves the central role of the gathering of the community in the Christian faith. The broadcast of the service of worship can be questioned in terms of its effectiveness (in both cost and in reaching nonbelievers) and its appropriateness for the Christian community.

109. Miller, p. 105.

110. Another approach to brevity is given by Robert Young, *Be Brief About It* (Westminster, 1980).

111. On festival days, the service tends to get overloaded with appeals for the special day offering, drama, dance, and music groups, especially planned but "extra" liturgical acts crammed into the service. The pastor dreams longingly of the big crowd and plans a grand, long sermon. These things, in addition to the difficulty of managing a large crowd, frequently combine to make the festival service seem cluttered and even disjointed. Listeners go away not so much refreshed by the living water but relieved that the service is over. The preacher, therefore, may find that the best sermon on a festival day is ten minutes long, focused like sunlight passing through a magnifying glass into a tiny, white-hot spot.

112. Van der Geest, pp. 40ff.

113. *Ibid., passim.*

114. Works that help with the delivery of the sermon include: Charles L. Bartow, *The Preaching Moment* (Abingdon, 1980); and Dwight Stevenson and Charles Diehl, *Reaching People from the Pulpit* (Baker, 1978, o.p. 1958).

115. In recent years, questions have been raised among churches that offer the weekly invitation about the adequacy of an invitation to which people may spontaneously respond. For example, is someone really prepared to make the confession that Jesus is Lord and to be baptized into a whole new life if (by chance) that person has heard only one sermon, albeit one that moved the person deeply? Is it fair to ask someone to join a congregation when they do not know all that is involved in its life? Is it not responsible to ask those who would become a part of the church (either by confession of faith and baptism or by transfer of membership) to receive an extended period of instruction in the Christian faith? Such arguments need to be taken seriously. However, the practice of offering the invitation will continue into the foreseeable future; if it is to be done, it needs to be done well. And there are good reasons for doing so. The weekly invitation dramatizes the nature of God as continually seeking us and offering grace and succor, and having arms that are always open. The weekly invitation dramatizes grace itself. One need not attend a membership class (much less pass a confirmation exam) to demonstrate one's worthiness to God or to the church. The positive response to the invitation is simply the first step in the Christian life. An acorn is not a fully developed oak tree, and neither is a person fresh from the waters of baptism a fully mature Christian. Both the tree and the Christian need to grow. (This is the point of the doctrine of sanctification.) The weekly invitation calls for the church to develop a strong and attractive program of Christian nurture especially geared to those who are beginning their lives as Christians and graded so as to lead them into ever fuller lives of response to God. In most congregations of the Christian Church (Disciples of Christ), for instance, those who make a formal entry into the body are then simply dumped into the general life of the congregation. Few congregations contain classes or materials for those who are new to Christian faith and life. A congregation can easily combine preparatory membership classes with the weekly invitation.

116. Some churches find it helpful to print a sentence in the bulletin explaining the purpose of the invitation and offering instruction regarding what to do if one wishes to respond publicly. But a printed notice cannot satisfactorily take the place of a warm, positive, personal invitation.

117. Theologians making extensive use of communication theory include: Charles H. Kraft, *Communication Theory for Christian Witness* (Abingdon, 1983); Clement Welsh, *Preaching in a New Key* (Pilgrim, 1974); and Myron Chartier, *Preaching as Communication* (Abingdon, 1981).

118. I am indebted to John E. McKiernan of the University of South Dakota for many of these suggestions.

DATE DUE

OCT 19 '86			

DEMCO 38-297